Preaching Through the Bible

2 Samuel

Michael Eaton

Sovereign World

Sovereign World
PO Box 777
Tonbridge
Kent TN11 9XT
England

By the same author:

Ecclesiastes (Tyndale Commentary) – IVP
The Baptism with the Spirit – IVP
How to Live a Godly Life – Sovereign World
How to Enjoy God's Worldwide Church – Sovereign World
Walk in the Spirit – Word
Living Under Grace (Romans 6–7) – Nelson Word
Preaching Through the Bible (1 Samuel) – Sovereign World

ISBN: 1 85240 173 7

Typeset by CRB Associates, Norwich
Printed in England by Clays Ltd, St Ives plc

Preface

There is need of a series of biblical expositions which are especially appropriate for English speaking preachers in the Third world. Such expositions need to be laid out in such a way that they will be useful to those who put their material to others in clear points. They need to avoid difficult vocabulary and advanced grammatical structures. They need to avoid European or North American illustrations. *Preaching Through the Bible* seeks to meet such a need. Although intended for an international audience I have no doubt that their simplicity will be of interest to many first-language speakers of English as well.

These expositions will take into account the Hebrew and Greek texts but will also take into account three translations of the Bible, the New King James (or Revised Authorized) Version, the New American Standard Version and the New International Version. The expositions will be comprehensible whichever of these three versions is used, and no doubt with some others as well. At times the expositor will simply translate the Hebrew or Greek himself.

It is not our purpose to deal with minute exegetical detail, although the commentator often has to do work of this nature as part of his preliminary preparation. But just as a good housewife likes to serve a good meal rather than display her pots and pans, so the good expositor is concerned with the 'good meal' of Scripture, rather than the 'pots and pans' of dictionaries, disputed interpretations and the like. Only occasionally will such matters have to be discussed. Similarly matters of 'Introduction' do not receive detailed discussion. A simple outline of some 'introductory' matters is to be found in 1 Samuel (pp. 124–127), and the appendix to this book refers to some books relating to 2 Samuel.

Michael A. Eaton

Contents

Contents

Author's Preface

Most of the material in this little book of mine was prepared for meetings of the Chrisco Fellowship of Churches in Nairobi in 1995. Worshippers in Nairobi City Hall lunchtime meetings, in Central Church, and other Chrisco venues, heard many of these chapters before anyone else. They are precious to me, and play a greater part in my writing and preaching than they realise.

Mrs Tina Gyaling worked on the last-but-one version of this material. Calvin has been an ever-present help in time of computer-trouble. Jenny and Carey and Trevecca tolerate (most of the time!) my tapping away on a computer at odd hours, for which I am grateful. Also to Mrs Florence Okumu who has helped keep this little book from being more difficult for the ordinary reader, and to Chris Mungeam of Sovereign World, an enthusiastic promoter and encourager – many thanks.

My greatest wish is that these books may encourage expository preaching. I stress both words: 'preaching' and 'expository'. Some preach like a thunderstorm – but say little. Others preach like an encyclopaedia but the people fall asleep and no lives are changed. I long for the balanced position: Spirit-filled expository preachers who are accurate when expounding the Scriptures and prophetic in applying them to the needs of the people. If my little book helps I shall praise God.

Michael A. Eaton

Chapter 1

Contentment in God
(2 Samuel 1:1–16)

David had been told by God that he would be king of Israel but he had learned in his early days to let God bring about his own promise in his own time and in his own way. So when Saul was killed David did not rush to secure his position as Israel's king.

The two books of Samuel teach us many lessons about God's kingdom. They were originally one book. At the beginning of the story the leadership of Israel was corrupt. God started a new venture in leadership with Samuel (1 Samuel 1:1–7:17) and soon it led to the demand for a king. However, Israel's first venture into kingship was a failure (1 Samuel 8:1–15:35) and God replaced Saul with David, a man after his own heart (Acts 13:22). David was a very human and fallible person. One of the reasons why he should be described as 'a man after God's heart' appears in this chapter. Under God's tuition David became incredibly willing to forgive everyone everywhere and leave his cause and his future entirely in the hands of God. This is what godliness is. This is what makes a man or woman a person after God's own heart.

At the end of 1 Samuel we have the story of how God chose David and put him through experiences of faith and of sufferings, all of which prepared him for the kingship (1 Samuel 16:1–31:13). Now, at the beginning of what we call '2 Samuel' the kingdom is at last to be given to David.

David was in Ziklag, his base (2 Samuel 1:1) when a man arrived from Mount Gilboa where Saul had been killed (1:2–3). He tells David about Saul's death (1:4) and claims to have helped Saul to commit suicide (1:5–10). It appears that the man is lying, because we know already that Saul committed suicide without help (1 Samuel 31:5). Apparently in the middle of the battle this man came across Saul's body and thought he had found an opportunity to tell a story which would be to his advantage. Or maybe he had been a witness to the events of 1 Samuel 31. Whatever may be the details, he thought he would be doing something wonderful in bringing Saul's crown and royal armlet to David. It would be evidence for David of Saul's death. To claim that he had been the one to finally bring about Saul's death would, he thought, be sure to get him some kind of reward from David.

The Amalekite was not prepared for David's response. David and his men show great grief (2 Samuel 1:11–12). David interrogates the man (1:13–14) and orders his execution (1:15–16).

Three principles emerge from the story.

1. **A leader has to learn generosity and forgiveness**. David is generous and forgiving in his grief-stricken reaction (2 Samuel 1:11–12). His grief is entirely genuine. The Amalekite could not conceive that David would be so truly sad at the death of a rival and enemy. But David had long before been taught to show nothing but love for his worst enemy, Saul. For years David had lived with Saul's hatred (see 1 Samuel 18, 19, 21, 23). *'Day after day Saul searched for him'* (1 Samuel 23:14), wanting to kill him. David had had opportunities to kill Saul (24:1–3) and had been pressed by his men to do so (24:4a). But he had come to regret even so small an act of hostility towards Saul as tearing his robe (24:4b–5) and had sharply rebuked his men for their hostility to Saul (1 Samuel 24:5–7). Later he not only spared Saul's life but rebuked Abner for failing to guard the king (26:15).

David had persistently supported Saul as the Lord's anointed and had even persuaded his men to feel the same way. At one stage they had wanted to kill Saul (1 Samuel

24:4a); but now *'all the men ... took hold of their clothes and tore them'*; they *'mourned and wept and fasted till evening for Saul'* (2 Samuel 1:11–12). David had taught his men well!

2. **A leader has to see justice done for everyone, including his enemies**. David was willing to see justice done for his one-time enemy (2 Samuel 1:13–16). The Amalakite who claimed to have killed Saul paid dearly for his lie. David was not delighted in the fall of Saul. Rather he protected the honour of Saul's name and wrought just revenge on the one who claimed to have killed him. Even a false claim to have killed Saul was instantly punished. David had no desire to gloat over the death of his old enemy. Rather he was generous and forgiving to him and took steps to see that someone who claimed to be his killer received summary punishment.

3. **A leader will be wise if he goes the second mile in love towards his enemies**. This is going to be one of the themes of the next few chapters. David takes steps to publicly honour Saul in a song of lamentation. He takes the trouble to compose a song and then orders that it should be taught to his own supporters. Saul was of the tribe of Benjamin. In demanding that the song should be learned by the people of **Judah**, David was showing great respect towards Saul but also insisting that his own supporters do the same. All of this shows us a man who had thoroughly learned to leave his entire life and future with God. In the history of God's people there has scarcely, if ever, been anyone who so thoroughly and totally showed love towards a terrible enemy. Saul had bitterly and viciously sought to kill David. If he had ever been able to catch David, David would have found no mercy and his death would have been certain. Yet David did not utter one word of this and treats Saul as his king and a hero of the nation.

Here is a man who has sufficient contentment and trust in God that he does not feel threatened by his predecessor. Nor is he panicky about who will be the next king. His personal ambition has been subjected to God's will. Here is a man of faith, of patience, a man without consuming personal ambition. A man prepared for kingship.

Chapter 2

A Gracious King

(2 Samuel 1:17–27)

It was a very gracious step when David took the time to compose a lamentation for his old enemy, Saul. Saul had for many years hunted David and kept him running all over the land. If he had caught him, David would have been killed without mercy. Yet David did not utter one word of this and treats Saul as his king and as a hero of the nation. He has nothing but praise for him. True, he says things of Jonathan that he cannot say of Saul. Saul could not be described as *'very dear to me'*, as could Jonathan.

The Hebrew of the song has difficulties in it but my own translation of it is as follows:

19a Your beauty, O Israel lies slain in the heights.

19b How the mighty are fallen!

20a Tell it not in Gath,

20b proclaim it not in the streets of Ashkelon,

20c lest the daughters of the Philistines be glad,

20d lest the daughters of the uncircumcised rejoice.

21a O mountains of Gilboa,

21b may you have neither dew nor rain,

21c nor fields that yield offerings.

21d For there the shield of the mighty was defiled,

21e the shield of Saul – no longer rubbed with oil.

22a From the blood of the slain,

22b from the flesh of the mighty,

22c the bow of Jonathan did not turn back,

22d the sword of Saul did not return unsatisfied.
23a Saul and Jonathan –
23b in life they were loved and gracious,
23c and in death they were not parted.
23d They were swifter than eagles,
23e they were stronger than lions.
24a O daughters of Israel,
24b weep for Saul,
24c who clothed you in scarlet and finery,
24d who adorned your garments with ornaments of gold.
25a How the mighty have fallen in battle!
25b Jonathan lies slain on your heights.
26a I grieve for you, Jonathan, my brother;
26b you were very dear to me.
26c Your love to me was wonderful,
26d more wonderful than that of women.
27a How the mighty are fallen!
27b The weapons of war have perished!

We may now comment on it as follows:

19a *'Your beauty'* is literally *'Your gazelle'* and refers to the swift-footedness of Jonathan. *'Slain in the heights'* alludes to Mount Gilboa which was in the hills.

19b In *'How the mighty are fallen'*, the Hebrew words are plural referring to Saul and Jonathan.

20a *'Tell it not in Gath.'* Gath was a Philistine town, a place which would be delighted to know of the death of Saul and Jonathan.

20b Ashkelon is another Philistine town.

20d *'The uncircumcised'* refers to the Philistines who were famous as a people who did not practise circumcision.

21c The word *'offerings'* means *'offering of grain'*. David is poetically cursing the place where a tragedy occurred.

21e Traditionally shields were anointed before battle.

22d *'The sword of Saul did not return unsatisfied'* means that Saul often killed many in battle.

23b *'In life they were loved and gracious'*. This was more true of Jonathan than Saul but David is taking trouble to speak well of the dead Saul.

23c *'In death they were not parted'*. Jonathan was loyal to his father despite his knowledge of his father's weaknesses.

24c David speaks of *'Saul, who clothed you in scarlet and finery'*. He takes it for granted that Saul was generous to his people with the spoils of victory.

26a David speaks of *'Jonathan, my brother'*. David and Jonathan were brothers by way of covenant relationship.

Several aspects of David's song are noteworthy.

1. **He speaks well of Saul and Jonathan**. Jonathan is said to be sure-footed (*'Your gazelle'*). They are both *'mighty'* and courageous (*'from the blood of the slain ... from the flesh of the mighty the bow of Jonathan did not turn back, the sword of Saul did not return unsatisfied'*). He reminds us of their popularity (*'in life they were loved and gracious'*), and speaks of Jonathan's loyalty to his father (*'in death they were not parted'*). He tells of their skill (*'swifter than eagles ... stronger than lions'*) and their generosity (*'who clothed you in scarlet and finery, who adorned your garments with ornaments of gold'*).

2. **He speaks of his grief at their deaths**. David dwells upon the details of how they came to die. He grieves over the place (*'heights ... Gilboa'*) and curses it (*'may you have neither dew nor rain, nor fields that yield offerings'*). He calls upon the girls of the nation to grieve with him (*'O daughters of Israel, weep for Saul'*). He goes over the details of how they are *'fallen ... fallen in battle ... slain on your heights'*. He grieves that their enemies should know their disgrace (*'Tell it not in Gath ... Ashkelon'*). He dwells upon the details of *'the shield of Saul ... no longer rubbed with oil'*.

3. **He specially grieves over a dear friendship which has come to an end**. *'I grieve for you Jonathan, my brother; you*

were very dear to me. Your love to me was wonderful, more wonderful than that of women'.

All of this speaks much for David's freedom from any grudge against an old enemy. It speaks of his wisdom in not antagonising supporters of Saul who will one day be his subjects when he becomes the ruler of the entire nation.

Chapter 3

Early Steps in Kingship
(2 Samuel 2:1–7)

David's base was in Ziklag. When he heard the news of Saul's death he first gave himself to carefully giving honour to the deceased king. At the same time he knew that the day was approaching when God's promise to him long ago would be fulfilled, that he would be the king of Israel.

At this point there were several needs of the hour.

1. **David needed to take steps to assume the kingship**. God had called him to kingship. Sooner or later he would need to take steps to take up the responsibility for leading the nation, especially in the great task of overthrowing the Philistines and regaining lost territory.

2. **David would need to overcome enemies and rivals**. It was inevitable after the bitterness of Saul towards him, and after he had seemed to identify himself with the Philistines, that not everyone in the land would want David to be the king. For several years prior to this time Saul had trained part of the nation to hunt David to death. It was unlikely that all of these people would now take easily to David as their king.

3. This also means that **David would need to unite a divided people**. He would need to win over those who did **not** like him at this point in the nation's history. The leader of a country may have enemies, but he still has to be the leader of the whole country including those who have not been his supporters. In the same way, the pastor of a church may have in his congregation those who (at the moment) wish he were not

their pastor. But he has to be the pastor of the whole congregation and must seek to bind together both his friends and his enemies – which is no easy task!

In all of this we can see principles of leadership that apply in any age of the church. They are also 'problems' that Jesus has! Jesus is also 'taking the kingship'. He has been enthroned already, and must reign until he has put all enemies beneath his feet. He must begin by being the king of his people.

Jesus too must overcome enemies and rivals within his church. Some within his professing church are more his enemies than his friends.

Jesus also is engaged upon the task where he will unite his people as one. Ephesians 4:13 predicts a day when the church of Jesus will come to the *'unity of the faith'*. Wonderful day! It has not come yet! The prayer of John 17:21 has to be answered in a way that is obvious to the world, and yet without human-centred manipulation.

But Jesus exercises his kingship through us. If Jesus is a second David, we too are to be little Davids, people who reign with Christ. The kind of challenges that came to David will come to all of Jesus' people, all who seek to extend his kingdom under him, all who seek to be kings. Jesus is the king of kings. We are the kings that Jesus is the king of!

So how does David set about this momentous task? We can watch him in the pages of Scripture and see how God leads his model king.

1. We notice first of all that **David retains a great deal of calmness**. He is not in a hurry. We read, *'Now it was after this that David enquired of the* LORD *... '* (2 Samuel 2:1). Haste is often a sign of self-will. When we are not sure that something is God's will but we want to do it regardless, we are generally in a hurry. But when we are sure we are in God's will, we can afford to wait for God's timing.

2. We notice that **he prayerfully sought God's guidance** (2 Samuel 2:1). A new phase of David's life required fresh guidance. David knew he was to be king. He might have felt that he did not need any special guidance. He might have thought that 'common sense' was enough for him to know

that he should now take steps towards securing the kingship that had been promised to him. It was also logical for him to make Hebron his base because he and his family came from that area. But he did not take it for granted that he knew God's will.

David wanted to be sure that he was doing things at God's speed. As momentous an occasion as this required fresh guidance from God. It was a major fault of Saul's kingship that he did not seek God in this way (1 Chronicles 10:14). David sought guidance through the Urim and Thummim (stones in the priestly jacket of the high-priest that could symbolise 'Yes', 'No' or 'No answer'). The result was that David was led to make Hebron the place where he should first establish his kingdom (2 Samuel 2:1) He took his family there (2:2) and the men of Judah joined him with their families also (2:3).

3. We notice too how **he was very peacefully disposed towards those who could be his enemies**. He was made king by the men of Judah (2 Samuel 2:4). But it was quite likely that supporters of Saul would not like this. The new king of Judah begins by winning over potential enemies. He is told of the men of Jabesh Gilead who were loyal to Saul and had honoured Saul greatly at the time of his death (2:5). David takes the initiative in seeking to win them over. He prays for them (*'May you be blessed...'* 2:6a), and promises them his favour (2:6b) and invites them to accept him as their king also (2:7). It is easy to make friends into enemies; the more difficult thing is to make enemies into friends. Jesus came to make his enemies (the human race) into friends. He too comes to those who have been among his enemies and he too asks them to accept him as their king. Those who are like Jesus will be similar. They will want to make their enemies into their friends.

Chapter 4

Faith Amidst Impossibilities

(2 Samuel 2:8–32)

If David hoped that his calmness, his prayerfulness and his
kindness towards the supporters of Saul would swiftly bring
him into his kingship over the entire nation, he soon discovered that he had a much larger task on his hands. Despite
David's graciousness he soon found a fierce conflict was in
progress.

1. **David has to face vicious personal ambition**. Some
enemies cannot be overcome. David did his best to win over
those who felt genuine attachment to Saul. But Abner had
reasons for not wanting to acknowledge the kingship of
David. Self-centredness and ambition for oneself are very
basic drives of the human personality. In a situation where
one can see the possibility of getting advantage for oneself, it
is amazing how one will become genuinely and powerfully
convinced that one ought to promote oneself! David had
been chosen for the kingship by God himself. This was generally known in the nation of Israel. But Abner had been the
leading general of the country for a long time and was Saul's
cousin (1 Samuel 14:50). He was the commander of the army
at the time of the incident with Goliath and had known David
since he was a young man (1 Samuel 17:55, 56). On one occasion when Saul was wanting to kill David, Saul and Abner
had been sitting side-by-side (1 Samuel 20:25). On another
occasion David had rebuked Abner for not protecting Saul
(1 Samuel 26:14–16). If David became king it was certain
Abner would lose his eminence and Joab was more likely to

become the commander than Abner. So Abner appoints another member of the family as king over large areas of the land of Israel (2 Samuel 2:8–9). It took David seven years before he was able to be king in his capital in Jerusalem. For two out of the seven years, Abner's puppet-king reigned (2:10–11).

2. **David had to face unspiritual followers**. Not only did David have to face the enmity of Abner, his own general whose name was Joab was a man whom David could not control. Joab was David's nephew, the son of his sister Zeruiah. He was one of three brothers, Joab, Abishai and Asahel, all of whom were valiant soldiers. Time would demonstrate that Joab was a skilful general. But David was not able to control him. Even in David's early days he regarded Joab as wicked (2 Samuel 3:34) and was complaining *'these men the sons of Zeruiah are too difficult for me'* (3:39). David later made use of Joab to murder Uriah (2 Samuel 11). Joab also murdered David's son Absalom (18:14) and he murdered Amasa who was Joab's rival in the army (2 Samuel 20:9–10). David made use of him but he was a ruthless killer, a career soldier with a taste for war, a man totally without David's sensitivity towards God and affection towards people.

Abner who was David's enemy and Joab who was David's supporter met at Gibeon. The aggressor was Abner. He had started the civil war and it was his suggestion that the war should be settled by a series of twelve hand-to-hand fights between twelve pairs of soldiers (2 Samuel 2:12–15). The style of fighting was that whoever was the quickest grabbed the other by the hair while thrusting forward a sword. But the twelve pairs were evenly matched. Soon all twenty-four were mortally wounded and died (2:16). The conflict was repulsive and inconclusive. It led to a general battle in which Abner's forces were defeated (2:17).

The three brothers Joab, Abishai and Asahel, all followed Abner, with Asahel running the fastest close behind Abner (2 Samuel 2:18–19). Abner was reluctant to strike back because he knew he would incur the lasting hatred of Joab if he killed one of the three brothers (2:20–22), but Asahel was persistent and Abner killed him with an unexpected backward stab of his spear (2:23).

The other two brothers continued the chase (2:24). At evening the two armies were facing each other (2:25). Abner, who was the initiator of the civil war, now asked that this phase of the conflict should be called off (2:26); Joab was planning to do so the next morning (2:27). Responding to Abner he calls off the fight (2:28) and Abner escapes to his headquarters (2:29). Joab had lost twenty men, including his own brother. Abner had lost three hundred and sixty. Joab also went back to his capital (2:30–32). The conflict had seen the loss of hundreds of men, some of whom knew each other.

They were 'brothers' in the same nation (2:26). David was discovering that kingship over Israel was not going to come to him without the most bitter of conflicts and disputes.

All of this reveals the greatness of the obstacles facing David. He might be peaceable, but Abner and Joab were bloodthirsty. The chances of David's being able to unite a divided people, seemed far away. How could he win over those who had been loyal to Saul with such enemies as Abner and such supporters as Joab? How can he ever be the leader of the whole country? What was happening was surely worsening the situation. Deep wounds and animosities would inevitably follow. Half of the nation would harbour resentments against the other half. Men who had known each other would hate each other, just as Joab now hated Abner.

David might well now think his life's calling to rule over a united Israel was a hopelessly lost cause. But all of this is typical of the life of faith. Often when one's life's task is nearing fulfilment and the purpose of God is about to take a leap forward, there come mighty obstacles in the way of God's will. The Christian seems to have the sentence of death within himself (see 2 Corinthians 1:9). At that point it is vital to go on believing. If God has laid upon us his calling he will not like it if we say *'We are not able to go up'* (as in Numbers 13:31). It is a time to refuse to be intimidated. By faith and patience the promises are to be inherited. God will deliver us. We shall come through. Only our faith has to be held firm.

Chapter 5

Persistent Faith

(2 Samuel 3:1–5:3)

David had been thrilled as a young man when Samuel had told him he would be king. He had no doubt envisaged a wonderful life in a palace. But how differently it had turned out. Now he faces the reality of what kingship for God involves. What an immense task it is. Civil war, mighty enemies, deep hatreds, a land ravaged by Philistines, cities lost, people divided! Is this what Samuel's one-time promise to David involved? It now seemed a totally impossible task. Surely David's calling was now ended? Whatever Samuel had promised seems to have been lost. It now seemed quite clear that there was no possibility of it ever coming to fulfilment. The situation was rather like that of the Israelites on the edge of the promised land when it was said by the unbelieving spies *'We are not able to go up'* (Numbers 13:31). But whereas the Israelites drew back in unbelief, David did not!

How did David overcome such great and mighty obstacles? In these chapters we do not find David doing very much at all! All of the frantic activity is being done by Abner and Joab. David did not ask for Joab's bloodthirsty ways. The two generals on each side were doing things that David would not approve of. How did David overcome such an immensely difficult situation blocking the way to the fulfilment of his life's call? Actually David did not do anything!

Often God calls us to be up and doing. Often what is needed in God's kingdom is energetic *'striving according to his power'* (Colossians 1:29) for the fulfilment of his will. But sometimes – just sometimes! – God calls us to stand still, refuse any fear, and watch the salvation of God come as we do nothing (see Exodus 14:13). This is the way it is here. Despite everything that is against David, as long as he stands still and refuses to panic the kingdom will come to him. And so it turned out! Terrible things happened, but none of them block the forward move of David towards God's will for his life. It was a time to do nothing, a time to stand still and see the salvation of God. Even terrible things which never should have happened were turned around by God. Far from hindering David's cause they actually worked to his advantage. God worked everything together for good. The war went on for a long time (2 Samuel 3:1). David was settled at Hebron and his family grew (3:2–5). David's persistent faith and refusal to give up his call began to prove worthwhile. By faith and patience he began to inherit promises.

1. **As David was persistently believing, an enemy changed sides**. Abner and his puppet-king quarrelled (2 Samuel 3:6–11) and as a result Abner offered to change sides (3:12)!

2. **As David was persistently believing, a small victory became a big victory**. One might think that Abner's offer was a great victory. Abner realised that his cause was getting weaker and offered to persuade Israel to change sides on condition that he was granted amnesty and the exchanging of covenant-oaths of mutual support between him and David. This might seem a great offer for David. One would think that David might be delighted at Abner's offer as the end of all his troubles. Actually David's answer was to say *'No – unless Michal is restored to me'*. He demanded that his former wife, and the daughter of Saul, should be returned to him (2 Samuel 3:13). His demand was met (3:14–16). There was nothing romantic about this. David was simply aiming for an even bigger victory than Abner was offering him. Instead of grasping immediately at what Abner was giving him, David aimed at something greater. It meant that Saul's family would be totally surrendering their claims to the kingship and were giving their family-member to David. It meant that David was inheriting Saul's kingdom as his son-in-law and

that his rights to the kingship were being freely recognised by the family of Saul. His faith and foresight turned a small victory into a decisive victory.

3. **As David was persistently believing, the people were persuaded**. David not only received the kingship by God's call; he received it by popular nomination as well (2 Samuel 3:17–22). David had the military energy to have conquered Israel. Joab had shown how it was possible to slaughter the forces of Abner. But David had instead waited patiently and eventually there came a mass movement in his favour.

4. **As David was persistently believing, God worked things together for good even in the most awful events**. Abner had helped David on the understanding that a covenant-relationship would come into being between them. Certainly Abner would have become the general of the new regime. Joab would have none of this. When he arrived he violently protested; he had his ambitions too and still was burning with hatred towards the murderer of his brother. Abner is brought back; Joab kills him (2 Samuel 3:23–27). It would seem inevitable that the murder will ruin the arrangements for the nation to come over to David's side. However it works quite differently. So energetic is David in denying any involvement in Abner's death (3:28–35) that the people are actually pleased with David's genuine and far-reaching grief over one of Saul's party (3:36–38).

Something similar happens to Ish-bosheth, the puppet-king. He himself loses heart (2 Samuel 4:1). He has two military commanders (4:2–3) who do nothing about a direct descendant of Saul who is crippled (4:4) and therefore incapable of being king. But they assassinate Ish-bosheth and bring his head to David (4:5–8). He shows he has no violent feelings towards any descendant of Saul, the murderers are executed (4:9–12a) and Ish-bosheth's remains are given an honourable burial (4:12b). All of this turns to David's advantage and all the tribes of Israel freely choose David as their king (5:1–3). David has stood still and he has seen the salvation of God.

Chapter 6

Achieving the Impossible
(2 Samuel 5:4–9a)

David is now thirty-seven years old (2 Samuel 5:4–5) and king of the whole nation. The next thing is to create a capital. If he stayed at Hebron, in Judah, or in a town occupied by one of the other tribes, he would be favouring one tribe at the expense of the others. There was however one city which was suitable: Jerusalem. It had been occupied by the Benjamites but they had lost it, and it was now ruled by Jebusites, a pagan people. Jerusalem looked impossible to capture but David felt called to take it for God.

1. **God has a habit of overthrowing sinful strongholds**. The Jebusites were utterly confident that their city could never be captured. Jerusalem was known for its strength. When Israel had first invaded the land it had come into the hands of the Benjamites (Joshua 18:21, 28), although the border of Judah went past its southern side (Joshua 15:8) and it was now occupied by the pagan Jebusites. It was impossible – so it was thought – to overthrow it. It had deep valleys on two sides, the Valley of Hinnom to the south, the Kidron Valley to the east. The walls of the city and these deep valleys made it very difficult to attack. Within the city was the *'stronghold of Zion'* (2 Samuel 5:7). The Jebusites were quite confident that their city could never be taken by any invader. *'And the king and his men went to Jerusalem, to attack the Jebusites who inhabited that locality. One of them said to David "You will not come in here. On the contrary,*[1] *even the blind and the lame will turn you away." He was thinking "David will never enter here"'* (2 Samuel 5:6).

This is typical of the thinking of the world. They somehow think they are so secure. How often the world has felt entirely confident that it could resist and even overthrow Jesus Christ. One remembers times when people have crusaded against the gospel with blistering attacks, or when they have ridiculed the Bible as 'superstition'. But the ridicule of the world means nothing and will soon be overthrown. One recalls how something similar to this ridicule had happened in the life of David before. When he was only a boy Goliath had *'looked at David'* and *'despised him'* (1 Samuel 17:42). David already had learned that those who despise God are near to falling. David did not react to the insulting language of the Jebusites. He simply persisted in faith to see that their sneers were brought to shame. Because they were God's enemies, they were his enemies. He had no personal animosity against them; David had given up that kind of bitterness. But he was determined that a town that opposed God would be overthrown. The modern Christian is the same. He does not *'wage war as the world does'* (2 Corinthians 10:3). The weapons of his warfare are not worldly weapons. Yet the insults that come to God and his people only deepen the Christian's resolve. These 'strongholds' can be anti-God political empires. They may be modern pagan philosophies. They can be worldly wisdom or demonic opposition. But none of these things need trouble us too deeply. *'We have divine power to demolish strongholds!'* (2 Corinthians 10:4).

2. **God can bring about unexpected victories**. David was not intimidated by the confidence of the Jebusites. Far from it. He actually captured the stronghold very speedily, not by military cleverness but by the surprising guidance of God! We read: *'But David did capture the stronghold, Zion, which is now "the city of David"'* (2 Samuel 5:7). The sneers of the Jebusites led David to seek something they would not expect. He was given a surprising idea from God. There was a tunnel which ran from the inside of the city to the outside, giving access to the spring of Gihon which was outside the city. (It was re-discovered in 1867 and can be seen today.) Part of it was vertical; it was at this point buckets were lowered to get

water. It was almost impossible to climb, so one would not normally think it could be used to give access to the city. God gave David the idea of getting his men not to attack the city from outside, but to go in as a small company of daring soldiers, climbing up the water-shaft and springing a surprise attack upon those defending the city. David had said on that day *'Anyone who strikes the Jebusites let him attack* [2] *through the water-shaft,* [3] *and let him attack the "lame and the blind", who are David's enemies'* (2 Samuel 5:8).

If we are in touch with God there will be times when God will lead us in surprising ways. If God is leading us, the impossible can sometimes be done in the twinkling of an eye. The Jebusites thought that David could spend years seeking to attack Jerusalem and it would never give way. But when God's guidance was followed it fell with a speed that could scarcely have been imagined. It became known as the 'City of David' (2 Samuel 5:9a).

Just as the earthly Jerusalem was captured by speedy conquest under the guidance of God, so Jesus' kingdom, his heavenly Jerusalem, was brought into being by speedy spiritual victory. After a speedy victory David then made Jerusalem his home. So Jesus speedily ridiculed principalities and powers (Colossians 2:15), set up a heavenly home for his people, and is now gathering his people into *'the Jerusalem which is above'* (Galatians 4:26). All his activities flow from there. It is his heavenly throne room from which he rules the church. The heavenly Jerusalem is his capital city by right of conquest.

Footnotes

[1] The Hebrew *ki 'im* after a negative may mean 'on the contrary' or 'rather'. See B.K. Waltke and M. O'Connor, *An Introduction to Biblical Hebrew Syntax* (Eisenbrauns, 1990), pp. 671–673.

[2] 'Water-shaft' seems to be the best translation. Mauchline's commentary, although not very constructive, compactly surveys the issues involved in this difficult passage.

[3] The Hebrew verb *naga'* may mean 'assault' or 'attack' (as in 2 Samuel 14:10).

Chapter 7

Jerusalem, City of Peace
(2 Samuel 5:9b–21)

In understanding the significance of Jerusalem, one must not get excited about the actual physical city. As the earthly headquarters of God's work it was used for centuries but its centrality came to an end in the first century and it has not since that time been very important in the spreading of the gospel. The spiritual symbolism of the city is more important. Jerusalem is a picture of heaven, and of the people of heaven. It is a picture of a place of secure fellowship. The king in his city among his people became a picture of the King in his heavenly city with his redeemed people.

God wanted David to have a headquarters, a capital city. Jerusalem was David's capital; the heavenly Jerusalem is God's capital. In the story of the church, different cities have been centres of Christian influence. In New Testament times, for a while it was Jerusalem. Then Antioch became more important; even in the book of Acts one can sense the fading of the importance of Jerusalem. Later other places became important: Rome, London, Canterbury, Geneva, and more recently Manila, Nairobi, Bangkok, Hong Kong. None of these is our 'capital city'. Our headquarters is heaven. Heaven is where our instructions come from, where our resources come from. *'The Jerusalem above is free; she is our mother'* (Galatians 4:26). Our reward is the heavenly city. By faith we enter it even now and find it to be a city of peace.

God wanted David to have a place that is beyond the reach of enemies. Jerusalem was almost invulnerable; similarly the heavenly Jerusalem is the home of God's people and is beyond defeat. The earthly Jerusalem was so secure it was famous for its peace. The very word 'Salem' means peace (see the point made in Hebrews 7:2). The meaning of the first part of the name 'Jeru-' is not certain but it probably means 'City of . . .'. Jerusalem is by name 'City of Peace'. Our heavenly Jerusalem is also a place of safety and of peace, a truly impregnable city.

We see six aspects of David's life in this part of his story.

First, David made his base secure and from a place of safety consolidated God's work. There was a part of the city known as the Millo. 2 Samuel 5:9b says *'David built all around from the Millo towards the house'*. 'The Millo' was a part of Jerusalem.[1] *'The house'* must have been his own temporary home. He would often withdraw to a stronghold within the city (as in 2 Samuel 5:17).

Secondly, David reaped the blessings of many years of preparation (2 Samuel 5:10). David had been in preparation for years. He had learned many lessons of faith and of forgiveness. He had persisted in days of great opposition from the Philistines, from Saul and from Saul's family. Years and years of persistent faith had brought him to where he now was. Now there was a time of reaping in his life. Those who sow, reap. So David grew in stature as God's king. In all of his ventures, God was blessing him.

Thirdly, David received unexpected practical blessings (2 Samuel 5:11). He was given a friend and admirer in Hiram, the king of Tyre. David had been consolidating the capital for God's kingdom. Now someone else builds him a house while he is working for God. He seeks God's kingdom and finds other things being added to him.

Fourthly, David learns that his great ministry was not for his own sake. God's choice of any one of his servants is not merely for the sake of that person. God chooses us to use us. He appoints us for the service of others. So David was made to know that he was being blessed for the sake of Israel (2 Samuel 5:12).

Fifthly, David continued in his polygamy (2 Samuel 5:13–16). In this he was following the practice of ancient kings. The story of Genesis 2 must have been available to David in one form or another. It could have told him of another approach to marriage which would have brought greater happiness to his own life if he had been able to follow it. The royal wives became a source of much trouble for David. Abigail shared his faith. Bathsheba was clearly close to him in later days. But Solomon, who went even further than David in this matter, chose pagan wives. Four of David's sons were to give him trouble. None of them came from a stable home background. But we must remember the situation of the day. God was not condemning him in this matter (see 2 Samuel 12:8).

Sixthly, David continued in a life of dependence on God. Soon he was attacked by the Philistines who tolerated David as king of Judah but were alarmed at his becoming king of all Israel. The Philistine invasions were a response to the anointing of David as king. When we are about to be used by God we can expect to arouse opposition. Suddenly the crisis comes. The Philistines spread out in the valley of Rephaim, not far from Jerusalem.

It is significant how David responds. He withdraws to a place of safety, 'the stronghold' within the city, and there he seeks God (2 Samuel 5:17). He asks for God's guidance (5:18) and is led to attack the Philistines (5:19–20). When attacked, he already had a prepared stronghold. He did not go out immediately. Rather he went to consult the Lord from a place of safety first.

God gave him victory and so decisive was the breakthrough it seemed like a bursting flood of water, and the place became known as 'Baal-perizim' (*'Lord of Breaking Through'*, 2 Samuel 5:20). David's victory demonstrated the feebleness of Philistine idolatry, for the Philistines had brought their gods with them to war. But the gods were powerless. Apparently they discovered their idols were not doing them any good and in the midst of the battle abandoned them as useless (5:21). David's victory had demonstrated the powerlessness of idolatry.

Footnote

[1] See *The International Standard Bible Encyclopaedia*, vol. 2 (Paternoster, 1982), pp. 1000–1001.

Chapter 8

Success and Failure
(2 Samuel 5:22–6:11)

One of the keys to understanding David is to note the times he
seeks guidance and the times he forgets to seek guidance. The
one brings success; the other brings failure.

First, we have here **an occasion when David sought God's
guidance**. The Philistines are confident in their strength and
they try again to destroy David before he becomes further
established as the king of all Israel (2 Samuel 5:22). David
again seeks guidance (5:23). It is notable that he did not
assume that he already knew what to do since it had
happened before! God's ways are varied and what he did last
time may not be what he will do this time. This time David
was told to attack them from the rear (5:23).

But to begin with, he had to wait. The Philistines had
brought a larger army than before. David and his men are to
wait behind some trees and let the Philistines march by. At a
certain point God will send a wind. The sound of the leaves
flapping at the tops of the trees will sound like the marching of
an army. The Philistines will also hear it and will imagine that
the Israelites have a mighty army (as they do since God is with
them!). It was like a later event when the Israelites were fighting the Arameans and there came the sound of a great army,
after which the Arameans fled for their lives (2 Kings 7:6).

Great victories are possible when God is leading. David's
army was a small one. Human strength would have made this
victory quite impossible. The numbers against them were too
great. But by following God's leading, David wins a victory

(2 Samuel 5:25). One is reminded of the situation at the very beginning of the church. Twelve men were to start the evangelisation of the world. Human resources made it entirely impossible. They were utterly dependent on God. When there came *'A sound from heaven like a rushing mighty wind'* (Acts 2:2) they were to rouse themselves and start winning the world.

The next story in Samuel forms a contrast to the one before. For now we have **an occasion when David failed to seek guidance**. After David had established his capital and had overcome the Philistines (2 Samuel 5:17–25), the next thing on his heart was to bring the Ark back to Jerusalem. In the days when the Tabernacle had been in the centre of the camp of Israel, the Ark symbolised experiencing the presence of God and being able to approach him. The different stages of approaching God (outside the tent, in the holy place, in the holy of holies) symbolised increasing nearness to God. The open courtyard spoke of being **outside** fellowship with God. God had to be approached via blood-atonement and cleansing (the altar and the laver). Then the first section of the tent had three things in it, all of which symbolised fellowship with God. It contained the table with bread on it, symbolising a fellowship meal with God. It had a seven-branched lampstand, symbolising the light of the Lord. It had a smaller altar for burning incense. Symbolically prayers were mixed with the incense provided by God.

Then there was a compartment further in, speaking of a greater degree of the blessing of God. There was the Ark, a box symbolising the presence of God. In front of the Ark [1] was a golden pot of manna (speaking of God's provision) and Aaron's rod (speaking of approaching God via the Aaronic priesthood which offered blood-sacrifices). Inside the Ark was the Mosaic law, but it was not visible. Symbolically, enjoyment of the presence of God was **not** hindered by the threatening law, because the law was covered by the mercy-seat where the blood of sacrifice was sprinkled.

The Ark itself was the centre of the entire symbolic representation of the presence of God. It symbolised God's holiness because the tablets of the law were known to be inside the Ark. It symbolised mercy because of the mercy-seat, a slab of gold on which blood had been sprinkled. The Ark was also a place of kingship, for God was **invisibly** enthroned there. And it was a place of worship, for at the end of the Ark statues of cherubim were standing in the posture of worship and of readiness to do God's will.

Generally the Ark was not to be carried at all. It was only to be carried from Egypt until the people found rest in the land. From that point onward it was to remain in the centre of the people of God. It was right that David should want it in Jerusalem, but the law had instructions as to how it should be carried. No one was ever allowed to look into it. To look directly at the law of God is to invite death.

So David gathers his soldiers (2 Samuel 6:1). It was natural for David to do this. He was himself a soldier. He was acting in the way that he knew. Since the days when he was treated by Saul as an outlaw and he had found refuge in the cave of Adullam (1 Samuel 22), he had had his men supporting him. But David had not consulted God and he was neglecting the Mosaic laws concerning the Ark (in Numbers 4:5, 6, 15; 7:9). It was meant to be covered from view (Numbers 4:5, 6). The law warned that if it were touched, death would follow (Numbers 4:15). It was to be carried by the sons of Korah, not by soldiers (Numbers 4:15; 7:9). David was making some bad mistakes. He neglected God's written word, and neglected to consult the Lord, and he was using soldiers not priests. Soldiers were notable for their worldly strength. Levites were famous for their spiritual ministry. God's work gets done and God's presence comes to us when his work is being carried by spiritually minded people. The rest of the story (2 Samuel 6:2–12) tells of the disaster that followed.

Footnote

[1] These items were not inside the Ark, as is often thought. 'Before the LORD', Exodus 16:33, and 'before the testimony', Numbers 17:10 mean 'in front of the Ark'. Hebrews 9:4 should be translated *'having a gold pot . . . '*, not *'inside which was a golden pot . . . '*.

Chapter 9

Failure and Success Again
(2 Samuel 6:1–23)

A third mistake of David was to follow the ways of the world. Some years before, the Philistines had had to get the Ark back to Israel and they had used a cart (1 Samuel 6). David was copying the Philistines! They were the very people he had just defeated. But now he was doing the work of God in a Philistine manner! We not only have to defeat Philistines; we also have to avoid doing things in the manner of the Philistines.

David went with the bulk of the populace supporting him (2 Samuel 6:2). David was a natural leader and wanted to involve the people in what he was doing. Unfortunately at this point he was leading them into wrong ways.

They make a new cart (6:3). They feel that nothing but a specially made cart is appropriate for the Ark of the Lord. But it is worldly wisdom; it is not following God's written instructions. They bring down the Ark (6:4); every one is celebrating (6:5). People can feel very worshipful even when they are making a bad mistake. Suddenly the cart seems to shudder. Uzzah puts out his hand to steady the Ark (6:6) and is instantly killed (6:7). Rough territory of Israel was not good ground for carrying an Ark on a cart. God knew what he was doing when he demanded the priests carry it with poles. David is upset with God (6:8) and afraid (6:9). The Ark is left at a nearby house, the house of Obed-edom (2 Samuel 6:10–11).

The God who can *'break forth'* in giving victory can also

'break forth' in judgement. (Compare *'Baal-perizim'*, *'Lord of Breaking Through'*, in 5:20, with *'Perez-uzzah'*, *'Breaking Out Against Uzzah'*, in 6:8.)

When we are dealing with the holy presence of God much care and wisdom is needed. A mass of ignorant soldiers were not the right people to do this work at all. David neglected the instructions of the Mosaic law, and failed to consult God. The Ark spoke of the holy presence of God. It is quite impossible to approach God directly. He has to be approached by blood-sacrifice. There is no getting close to God without the blood of Jesus, and (in Old Testament times) there was no approaching the Ark without priesthood and blood-atonement.

For a while David gives up and the Ark remains abandoned at the home of Obed-edom, but then David comes to know that Obed-edom is being richly blessed. Where there is the presence of God, there is blessing (2 Samuel 6:12).

David had learned something about the dangers of God's presence. He had tried dealing with God **directly** without priesthood and the blood of atonement. No one could deal with God in ancient Israel without priesthood and blood-atonement. Similarly, today, no one can approach God without Jesus as his great high-priest and without the atoning blood of Jesus Christ.

But David discovers he needs the presence of God in his life and in his kingdom. He is fearful of the presence of God, yet he knows that he needs it and wants it. Where the Ark is – symbolising the presence of God – there is fullness of blessing. The Ark had been left at the house of Obed-edom. Now Obed-edom was being blessed personally and in his family and in his entire life because the presence of God was with him (2 Samuel 6:12). So David went and got the Ark and discovered this *'fullness of joy'* for himself. He brought up the Ark to his own headquarters *'with rejoicing'* (6:12).

But this time he did it more carefully.

1. This time it was carried by *'bearers'* (6:13), following the directions of the written Word of God.

2. There were sacrifices representing blood atonement. Every six steps they would stop and offer a sacrifice. We

experience the return of God's presence as we do all that we do, trusting only in the blood of Jesus.

3. David was dancing with exuberant joy. Before he had been angry and afraid (6:8–9). Now he is radiant with joy (6:14). It always brings great joy when we have put something right and when we know we are walking in the ways of God.

4. There was the ephod representing submission to the guidance of God (2 Samuel 6:14). It was a jacket with stones in it which could be used to tell the will of God. David wanted to express his willingness to submit to God's will and God's ways, so he wore the ephod which was one of the ways of guidance.

5. The presence of God was accompanied by noisy worship (2 Samuel 6:15). There is very little worship in the Bible that is quiet and dignified! There had been worship before (6:5). So the fact that there is noisy worship did not prove that a thing was right. But now the worship is true worship; they are truly walking in God's ways. David's wife, Michal, had no taste for such worship (6:16)! Her idea of kingship was dignified and proud. She had no interest in being married to a king who joined in with the people and threw aside his dignity.

6. The presence of God brought national blessing. David put the Ark in a tent (6:17) and offered sacrifices symbolising consecration and fellowship through the blood of sacrifice. He prayed for the people (6:18) and provided for them physically (6:19) and the entire nation was blessed. Only Michal was unhappy (6:20). She had no interest in the presence of God, no taste for worship. But David is not moved even by a disunity at the most sensitive part of his life, his relationship with *'the wife of his youth'*. He lets nothing distress him! He knows that he has been chosen by God and knows that he has good reasons to rejoice (6:21). He knows that what he has done is right and that others will appreciate him even if one who had been close to him in days gone by does not (6:22). Michal loses by her unspirituality (6:23) but David continues steadfast. No matter what comes our way, even the deepest disappointment, we are to *'be steadfast, immovable'* (1 Corinthians 15:58).

Chapter 10

Freedom and Guidance

(2 Samuel 7:1–7)

The work of the Lord has a lot to do with sowing and reaping. David has been serving the Lord amidst great conflicts for many years. Now he comes to a time of great blessing and to a spiritual breakthrough of the highest kind.

1. **David has shown faithfulness in persisting in well-doing for many years**. David is in a peaceful time of his life (2 Samuel 7:1) and is about to reap a great blessing. But this peaceful time has a lot to do with the great struggles he has been through in previous years. He has been serving the Lord for many years now. He had been growing in skill in his leadership of men. He had organised his army and had often led them into battle. He had given his attention to building Jerusalem and had brought the Ark there.

2. **David has more spiritual ambitions for God's kingdom**. David had a concern in his heart to provide a better housing for the Ark of God (2 Samuel 7:2). As it turned out, God was about to veto David's plan. But it was not wrong for David to have spiritual desires. There are plenty of worldly people who have plans and ambitions about their businesses, their financial prosperity, the success of their children. Why should God's people not have hopes and wishes for the progress of God's kingdom and God's work? Paul had longings and desires in his work for the Lord. He could say to the Christians at Rome *'I long to see you so that I may impart to you some spiritual blessing'* (Romans 1:11). He could say *'If any*

one has set his heart on being an overseer, he desires a noble task' (1 Timothy 3:1). The woman of Matthew 26:6–13 poured her perfume over Jesus' head without special instruction and Jesus commends her (Matthew 26:10). It was something she wanted to do.

God gives us a lot of freedom. Nathan does not rebuke David but tells him to follow his spiritual desires (2 Samuel 7:3). Often the calling of God comes along the lines of what we want to do for God. Generally it is good to cautiously follow our spiritual instincts and longings. David is enjoying a restful time in the work of the Lord but he uses this time to be thinking of yet more things he can do for God. He is a person who always likes to be finding new things to do for God. God likes a *'willing mind'* (2 Corinthians 8:12). Although God turned down David's offer he approved of it and said to him *'You did well'* (1 Kings 8:18).

3. **David had to be open to God's overruling**. It had seemed good both to David and to Nathan to plan to build the temple for God's Ark. But although God gives us a lot of freedom and we live under a law of liberty (James 1:25), yet we have to be ready for God to overrule and guide us other than in the way we were planning. That night Nathan receives a revelation (2 Samuel 7:4). God did not reject the idea of building a temple altogether but he questioned whether David was the right person to build it (7:5). God has been quite content to have a movable shrine (7:6). God has never given any instruction about a temple (7:7).

For much of the time God gives us freedom. We do not need to seek to know God's will for every tiny detail of life. We must not think of life as following a minutely detailed schedule where we have to ask God to discover what is on the hidden agenda. The godly men and women of the Bible did not live that way. Most of the time God gives us freedom and expects us to use good judgement following the principles of scriptural teaching and scriptural wisdom. David did not spend hours asking for guidance about every detail of his life. He had his own desires and he had good judgement.

Yet we have to ask God what his desire is. David did this in sharing with Nathan what was on his heart for God's work. He was asking 'What is God's will?' not in the sense of 'What is on the hidden agenda?' but in the sense of 'What is God's wish about this particular matter that is on my mind?' Although God gives us a lot of freedom, we consult him as we use our own good judgement. We ask him for confirmation. Major decisions should be prayed over. God has the right to overrule our hopes and desires. Both Nathan and David were using their God-given freedom in seeking the best for God's kingdom. But they both had to face the fact that God has some opinions of his own. God has a will for our lives. It must not be thought of as a hidden agenda but as a wish that he has right now.

Most of the time the godly men and women of the Bible are not being given direct and minute guidance. Most of the time they are expected to use their judgement. When in Acts 15:36 Paul says *'Let us go back and visit the brothers'*, he is using God-given freedom. On another occasion *'Paul had decided to sail past Ephesus'* (Acts 20:16). He was following sensible reasons. He wanted *'to avoid spending time in the province of Asia'* and he was *'in a hurry to reach Jerusalem, if possible by the day of Pentecost'*. The godly people of the Bible use their mind and their good judgement. David wanted to build a temple. He was enjoying his God-given freedom.

But when we need special help we get it, and God has his desires too. So David is overruled. God trains us in ways of wisdom and good judgement. But from time to time we need special help and we get it. We enjoy our freedom. We use our judgement. We spend time in prayer. We consult with good counsellors. And we expect God to guide.

Chapter 11

The Temple

(2 Samuel 7:5)

God did not reject the idea of having a temple for his Ark, but he questioned whether David was the right person to build it (2 Samuel 7:5). God had been quite content to have a movable shrine (7:6) and had never given any instruction about a temple (7:7).

The temple will be built, but it will be Solomon not David who builds it. Some people get greedy in the work of the Lord. They want to do everything! But some things have to be left for the next generation.

What exactly is 'the temple' all about? **It incorporates all of the ideas of the Tabernacle and yet it goes beyond the Tabernacle.** The Tabernacle was a movable tent. The later temple in Jerusalem had the same kind of basic shape but it was a solid building and not movable.

The Tabernacle and the temple both symbolised experiencing the presence of God. God's great purpose is to dwell with us and that we should dwell with him. In the Old Testament the Tabernacle and the temple were ways of symbolising this. God was present within his people. Yet because of human sin the glory of God was 'located' inside the holy of holies. Men and women are too sinful for the holy presence of God to be among them visibly and gloriously in every place. It would be too terrifying. His holy presence would kill anyone who had contact with it. So God's presence was 'confined' to the holy of holies, the innermost room of the Tabernacle. The way into

41

the presence of God was only for the high-priest. He could go there only once a year and he had to take the blood of sacrifice as he went in. God's glory remained hidden. It was known by faith but was not directly experienced. The Ark was the centre of the place where God revealed himself in glory. The actual visible presence of God was located just above the Ark. The Ark itself was a 'throne' for God the King.

In the New Testament, 'temple' is a picture of God's indwelling. The church is God's new temple (2 Corinthians 6:16–7:1; Ephesians 2:20–22). The earthly temple in Jerusalem was a picture of God's heavenly church. Right now the Christian is a member of the heavenly city, the heavenly Jerusalem (Hebrews 12:18–24). A temple in the ancient world was the place where God lived and manifested himself. The equivalent in our thinking is the church and heaven – the same thing because the church is already spiritually in heaven in the presence of her king, the Lord Jesus Christ. The temple was God's palace (the Hebrew word means 'palace' and 'temple' at the same time; there is no difference). At the end of the Bible when we have predictions of the end of the world and the old world is abolished, *'the holy city, the new Jerusalem'* comes down. The real 'Jerusalem' is heaven. At the end of the world it comes down and there is heaven on earth (Revelation 21:1–2). In the new Jerusalem there is *'no temple in the city, for its temple is the Lord God'* (Revelation 21:22). There is no temple because the whole city is temple! God himself will be visible and glorious. The whole *'new Jerusalem'* is the sanctuary, the dwelling place of God.

In the story of 1 and 2 Samuel we have the account of how the Ark was misused and how its dwelling-place at Shiloh became the centre of the sin of Israel. Now David is wanting God to be at the centre of the life of Israel. He wants God to be 'enthroned' in a palace. The difference between the picture-language of 'tabernacle' and the picture-language of 'temple' is that the temple always imagines a **settled** situation. This chapter begins by telling us God had given David *'rest'* from his enemies.

God gives three reasons why David should not be the one

to build it. The first reason is that **the temple is associated with peace**. Before this time, God and Israel had been 'on the move'. There has been no 'rest' in the relationship between God and his people for a long time. But now things are changing. God is now, more than before, coming into the centre of the life of Israel. This had not been true during the days of the judges or during the time of Eli and of Saul. Now God has got his king – David. God has got his capital – Jerusalem. God has got his Ark there. There have been many victories. The nation is *'entering into rest'* (see 2 Samuel 7:1). Soon it will be right to build a temple, a picture of the **settled** presence of God among his people. It would be a symbol of God's ruling in his people. The Ark was his throne. The holy of holies was his throne-room. However, David's life had been a life of great military conquests. It was not appropriate that a soldier and war-hero should build the temple. God thought one who had had to take so many lives should not be the builder of a symbol of peace and rest. *'Are you the one?'* asked God. David has been the builder of an earthly empire. But it will be a *'prince of peace'*, Solomon, who will build a sanctuary, a temple, a place of peace.

Jesus is of course both the fulfilment of the David-picture and the fulfilment of the Solomon-picture. He is the Mighty Conqueror and he is also the Prince of Peace. He has a temple for us. Our temple is heaven but we have something of it already. We have already come to our heavenly Jerusalem. We are not at Mount Sinai (Hebrews 12:18); we are on Mount Zion (Hebrews 12:22). We are God's temple. He lives within us. One day we shall have a 'temple' in an even greater way. The heavenly Jerusalem will be heaven-on-earth. There will be no temple within the city, because we shall be in the holy of holies all the time!

Chapter 12

Entering Into Rest

(2 Samuel 7:6–17)

A second answer to David's suggestion that he should build a temple is that **God has been quite content to have a movable shrine for his Ark**. *'I have not dwelt in a house from the day I brought the Israelites up out of Egypt to this day'* (2 Samuel 7:6). God had never given any instruction about a temple (7:7). God is quite happy to be a nomad! It is men and women who like permanent structures, cold and motionless buildings, steadily operating machines, long-standing traditions. God likes pilgrims and tents. He is always on the move. His Holy Spirit is like the uncontrollable wind, like lubricating oil.

The temple is only a symbol. God is more concerned about the reality of his spiritual work than a symbolic building. Even when the temple was built Solomon said *'the highest heaven cannot contain you'* (1 Kings 8:27).

This leads on to the third answer given to David. God is more concerned to build David a house than for David to build a house for God's Ark. God actually proposes to do something wonderful for David, and he reveals his plans for David here.

God summarises the blessings David already has. (1) God had chosen him (2 Samuel 7:8). Every one of God's people is 'elect'. God has chosen us, taken us out of where we were, in the kingdom of darkness. He has for us a calling. In David's case it involved the end of his days as a shepherd, and his being placed as leader of Israel. It was all God's doing. Something similar is true of every believer. *'He chose us in Christ . . . to the praise of the glory of his grace'* (Ephesians 1:4, 5).

(2) God had given David his presence (2 Samuel 7:9a). *'I have been with you wherever you went'*. All those years when David was escaping Saul, running here and there in the wilderness, training a small army, preparing for the days of kingship, enduring trials of all kinds, all those years God had been with him. He promises never to leave or forsake his people. He says again and again *'I will be with you'*.

(3) God had given David his protection (2 Samuel 7:9b). *'I . . . have cut off all your enemies . . . '*. How many times God had protected David when Saul was so close or when Goliath stood in front of him or when Philistines were assembling their armies against him. God had never let him down and had rescued him again and again.

Now God promises to do even more. He proposes to give David a great name (2 Samuel 7:9c), a land for Israel (7:10), freedom from oppression (7:10b–11a), rest from enemies (7:11b). David himself will be given a household (7:11c–12). David's son will build the temple (7:13a) and will have an eternal dynasty (7:13b). God will be a father to him; he will be a son to God (7:14a). If he sins he will be chastised (7:14b) but God's love is given to him on oath and cannot be lost (7:15). The kingdom will be an eternal kingdom (7:16). Through Nathan this revelation (7:17) is given to David. The fact that it comes through Nathan is a hint that David must allow prophetic ministry to be alongside him as all of this comes to pass. It involved a prophet from its earliest point.

These verses are one of the great highlights of the Bible. It is the time in David's life when he *'inherits the promises'* (Hebrews 6:12), experiences God's oath and *'enters into rest'*. It was the time when he was given a *'covenant of generosity'* and God swore to him an unconditional oath of blessing that can never be forfeited. It was the time in his life when he *'entered into rest'*.

This phrase *'enter into rest'* was used by David himself in

Psalm 95:11, and it was used in the letter to the Hebrews (Hebrews 3:11, 18; 4:1, 3, 5, 11).

To *'enter into rest'* is the reward that comes to the Christian in this life as a result of his diligent faith. It is the joy of inheriting promises. It is experiencing the oath of God's mercy. It is when after years, maybe, of persistent faith, we come to have an assurance that we have obtained that which we have been looking for and which God has promised us.

'Entering into rest' is what happened to David when after years of trials and tribulations he finally came to the point where God took an oath, and without the possibility of any reversal said to David *'Your seed will continue for ever. I swear it!'* (see especially Psalm 89). On God's side an oath was taken. On David's side after many struggles against many enemies *'The Lord had given him rest on every side'* (2 Samuel 7:1) but also gave him rest within by giving an unshakeable oath that his seed would last for ever.

This chapter is the record of an oath (as is clear because of 2 Samuel 7:15 and abundantly clear because of Psalm 89). What is happening when God takes an 'oath'? There are places in the Bible where God is portrayed as changing his mind. God is able to withdraw his promises, if there is no persistent faith, and able to abandon his threats, if there is repentance. The stories of Nineveh in the book of Jonah and of Saul in 1 Samuel are examples. God may amend his purpose if an oath has not been taken. The oath of God is the **point where God 'makes up his mind' and the point after which God will not change his mind**. Thus after the decision of God that Saul should be rejected it is said of God *'he is not a man that he should repent'* (1 Samuel 15:29); this takes place **after** Saul has persistently failed in obedience and God has *'made up his mind'* about Saul. It is also said of the priest after the order of Melchizedek *'Yahweh has sworn, **and will not repent**'*. The oath is the point at which a decision is made as to whether the promises will in fact be inherited. At this point David receives the oath. He enters into rest.

Chapter 13

All Things Are Yours
(2 Samuel 7:9b–11a)

In the middle of verse 9 the tense changes. David is told (via Nathan) of what God has done. Now God gives an oath concerning what he will do. The proof that 2 Samuel 7 records an oath to David is Psalm 89. 2 Samuel 7:15 is also clearly the language of an oath. When we discover something that is said to be irreversible ('*I will not take my steadfast love away from you as I took it away from Saul*') we have an indication that we are dealing with oath and covenant. Psalm 89 puts the matter beyond doubt; it speaks of covenant and oath in these promises to David (Psalm 89:3, 28, 34, 49).

What happens in 2 Samuel 7 is the equivalent in David's life to what happened to Abraham according to Genesis 22. After years of diligent faith and testing, God'said to him '*Now I see that you fear me*' (see Genesis 22:12) and took an oath (Genesis 22:16). At that point **on God's side** an oath was taken. At that point **on Abraham's side**, he entered into rest. At that point the promise was '*obtained*'. Promises had been given to Abraham for many years; they were to be inherited by faith and patience. Obedience is required if they are to come to full fruition. They could have been aborted as happened in the case of Saul. Then comes a test (Genesis 22:1); Abraham passes the test by responding in faith and obedience. At that point God takes the oath concerning the promises. God has 'made up his mind' about Abraham. From now on, the purposes of God are immutably fixed with regard to the *'seed of Abraham'*. The promised seed will bring international blessing through Abraham's line. The land of Canaan will indeed be given to Abraham's people.

There are four major occasions in the Old Testament when God takes an oath: the oath to Abraham (Genesis 22:16), the oath taken in anger concerning the forfeiting of the land of Israel for the first generation of Israel (Numbers 14:20–23), God's oath to the Davidic dynasty (Psalm 89:19–37), and his oath concerning the Messianic priest-king (Psalm 110:1–4).

What we are seeing here is God's oath to David concerning the promises to him. This is the meaning of *'entering into rest'*. It is the reward that comes to the believer in this life as a result of diligent faith, the joy of inheriting promises and experiencing the oath of God's mercy.

What are the promises that have been 'inherited' at this point?

1. **He swears to give David a great name**. *'I will make for you a great name like the name of the great men on the earth'* (2 Samuel 7:9c). *'A name'* is one of the great promises of the Bible. God said to Abraham *'I will make your name great'* (Genesis 12:2). Everyone deep within wants to be known and remembered. The builders of the tower of Babel said *'Let us build a city ... so that we may make a name for ourselves'* (Genesis 11:4). God's judgement for sin includes abandoning the person to such oblivion that not even his name is remembered. The wicked Canaanite kings were to be destroyed and God told Israel *'you will wipe out their names'* (Deuteronomy 7:24). When Israel sinned God threatened *'I will destroy them and blot out their name from under heaven'* (Deuteronomy 9:14). God rewards by giving a name. The godly men of Isaiah 56:4 were told *'I will give to them within my temple and its walls, a memorial and a name ... I will give them an everlasting name that shall not be cut off'* (Isaiah 56:5). One part of reward for godly people is to be given an everlasting name. *'Your name ... will endure'* (Isaiah 66:22). The reward for diligent faith is amongst other things to be given a good standing. David will gain honour in the eyes of people because of his diligence.

David also prefigures Jesus, God's supreme king over his people. Part of Jesus' heavenly reward was that God highly exalted him and gave him a name (Philippians 2:9). He was exalted *'above every name that is named'* (Ephesians 1:21).

The blessing of 'a name' is also offered to believers who persist in diligent faith. *'To him that overcomes . . . I will give a new name'* (Revelation 2:17). *'Him that overcomes . . . I will write on him my new name'* (Revelation 3:12). *'His name shall be on their foreheads'* (Revelation 22:4).

2. **God swears to give through David a land for Israel**. *'I will appoint a place for my people Israel, and will plant them, so that they may dwell in their own place. They will not be molested again, nor will they again be afflicted by wicked people as they were before* (2 Samuel 7:10), *from the day I appointed judges over my people'* (7:11a). For Israel and David this was quite literal. For David's sake, God gave Israel security within the land. This did not mean that any one generation could guarantee dwelling in the land. Sin could result in temporary removal, as in the days of Babylonian exile. But the land would come back to them, Jeremiah would echo this promise when they were in exile, *'I will gather them out of all the lands . . . I will bring them back to this place and make them dwell in safety'* (Jeremiah 32:37). God gave a physical territory to the people of Israel. Until the coming of Jesus it was quite literal.

Jesus is the fulfilment of the promise. David was simply a shadow of Jesus. Jesus is the one who is given the world (including Israel but the promise is widened). He is the *'heir of all things'* (Hebrews 1:2).

The Christian is *'heir with Christ'*. The spiritual equivalent to this promise is what Paul would call *'possessing all things'* (2 Corinthians 6:10). It is what Paul refers to in 1 Corinthians 3:21–23. There is a spiritual equivalent to *'inheriting the land'*. It is satisfaction with God's world, *'possessing all things'*, knowing that all things are ours. It is a sense of belonging in God's world, security in God, inclusion in God's people, happiness in being given responsibility by God. *'All things are yours . . .'*.

49

Chapter 14

The Promises to David

(2 Samuel 7:11b–16)

God swore to give through David a land for Israel. There is a spiritual equivalent today. Jesus said that any Christian who had suffered the loss of earthly blessings for his sake will *'receive a hundredfold now in this age, houses and brothers and sisters and mothers and children and lands, with persecutions, and in the age to come eternal life'* (Mark 10:30). The meek inherit the earth (Matthew 5:5).

One day it will be quite literal again, because a *'new heaven and new earth'* is promised to the people of God. The *'seed of David'*, Jesus, and all of his people will have in the new heavens and new earth *'a place for my people'* and in a fuller sense than ever will *'dwell in their own place'* and will be beyond the reach of all enemies.

3. **God swears to give, through David, rest from enemies**. *'Also I will give rest to you* (singular) *from all your enemies'* (2 Samuel 7:11b). In this promise 'rest' does not mean an easy or lazy life. David had further battles to fight including some from his own family. 'Rest' means rather that a period of uncertainty is completed and the promise is secured. In **this** sense David has *'entered into rest'*. It means the promise of the conquest was achieved. The promise had been secured that Israel had definitively been given the land. It was 'rest' in the sense that the issue was not in doubt.

4. **God promises to give David himself a household**. *'Also the Lord declares to you that he will make a "house" for you'*

(2 Samuel 7:11b). *'When your days are fulfilled and you lie down with your fathers I will raise up your seed after you, someone who will come from your loins, and I will establish his kingdom'* (7:12). The promise was fulfilled in Solomon (see 1 Kings 8:20).

5. **He swears that David's son will build the temple**. *'He shall build a house for my name'* (2 Samuel 7:13a).

6. **God swears that David's son will have an eternal dynasty**. *'I will establish the throne of his kingdom for ever'* (2 Samuel 7:13b).

7. **God swears that there will be a father–son relationship between God and David's son**. *'I shall be a father to him and he shall be a son to me. If he sins I will chastise him with a rod of men and with strokes from the sons of men* (2 Samuel 7:14). *But my kindness shall not depart from him as I took it away from Saul whom I removed before you'* (7:15). God will be a father to Solomon, protecting him, providing for him, guiding him. Solomon would be a son to God, presenting him, furthering his plans in this world. The fact that this father–son relationship could never be broken (since it was the subject of an oath) meant that extreme measures might have to be taken to keep his son in the ways of obedience. This was sobering, but the other side of the coin was that there was no question of God's love ever being withdrawn. It could never be withdrawn because an oath had been taken. Psalm 89:30–37 makes it utterly clear. Not even serious sin will make God change his mind, now that the oath is taken. Actually David did fall into extreme sin (in connection with Bathsheba and Uriah's murder) but it did not stop God's purpose. Indeed, Solomon was the son of Bathsheba!

8. **The kingdom will be an eternal kingdom**. *'Also your house and your kingdom shall be established for ever before me. Your throne shall be established for ever'* (2 Samuel 7:16).

How were these prophecies to be fulfilled? It started with David. David was given a great name and the land was thoroughly secured through him. He *'entered into rest'* with regard to the promises to him.

Then came Solomon, David's son. He was David's seed.

He built the temple. But the predictions go further still. David and Solomon were promised an eternal house and an eternal kingdom. The various sons of David, the kings in David's line, were all failures to a lesser or greater extent. So it became clear that only a very unique 'Son of David' could fulfil all these hopes.

The prophets began to expect a new 'David' (Ezekiel 34:23). The psalmists looked forward to a King who would bring an everlasting kingdom. Isaiah tells Ahaz about a child to be born in the house of David whose name is *'the mighty God'* (Isaiah 7:14; 9:6–7). Jeremiah knows that God will raise *'a Branch'* out of the house of David (Jeremiah 23:5–6; 33:14–17).

These promises can only be fulfilled in a much greater 'David' than David! Jesus was the one in view. Like David he is a man of God's choice. Like David he did his work in the anointing of the Holy Spirit. Like David he rules over the entire people of God. Like David he delivers his people from their enemies. Like David he does his work on behalf of the Father. He allowed people to call him *'Son of David'* (Mark 10:47–48; Matthew 15:22). Paul calls him *'Son of David'* (Romans 1:3; 2 Timothy 2:8). Luke points out that Jesus was born in the house of David (Luke 1:2–27); so does Matthew (1:1–16, 20). The angel told Mary *'God will give to him the throne of David'* (Luke 1:32–33). Zechariah gave thanks that in the events approaching the birth of Jesus there was *'salvation . . . in the house of his servant David'* (Luke 1:67–79). The angels rejoiced in a Saviour born in the city of David (Luke 2:10–11; also 2:1–5).

It is the work of Jesus to build a 'house', a spiritual 'temple'. Jesus' temple is the church. He builds it. The church is God's dwelling place in the Spirit (Ephesians 2:20–22). He was David's seed 'raised up' (in more than one sense) to establish God's kingdom. It is his throne that will last for ever. He is the Son to the Father, and the Father is his Father (see how Hebrews 1:5 quotes 2 Samuel 7:14). He is the one who represents the Father perfectly and furthers his kingdom in this world.

Chapter 15

Prayer and Organisation
(2 Samuel 7:17–8:18)

After the revelation given to David (2 Samuel 7:17), he responds with prayer (7:18a), expressing his unworthiness (7:18b–19), ascribing all his blessings to God's word (7:20–21), admiring God's greatness and uniqueness (7:22) and the marvel of what he has done for Israel (7:23–24). Then he turns the promise into prayer (7:25–26), asking for personal blessing upon his own household (7:27–29).

1. **David is humbled by the thought of God's sovereignty.** He refers to God as *'sovereign LORD'* (2 Samuel 7:18–20). God has shown sovereign graciousness to David. He feels unworthy. He has come such a long way since the days he was a shepherd-boy (7:18). It is all part of God's plan (7:19). God knows all about him, so David knows that God is not under the impression that David deserves any of this (7:20). The promises that have just come to David are a sign of God's prearrangement, and his faithfulness to his promises (7:21).

2. **He admires God.** God is great, immense in wisdom and kindness and magnificent plans. God is unique (2 Samuel 7:22) and has done a unique thing in his people, making them unique also (2 Samuel 7:23). God has acted as king, bringing redemption, release from bondage, glory for himself, justice towards the sins of the nations, banishment of sinful nations, exaltation of his own people (2 Samuel 7:23). He is acting sovereignly to bring about the creation of a people for himself (2 Samuel 7:24).

3. **David prays for the promise to be fulfilled**. God likes his servants to claim his promises. *'Do what you have promised'*, he says (2 Samuel 7:25). But his prayer begins by asking for the honour of God's name (7:26). He is bold to pray because God has given his word (7:27). He is pleading promises – always the secret of prayer (7:28). He pushes his request as high as it can go. He asks for **eternal** blessings. God had promised them for ever. So David asks for them to last for ever. His faith is as big as the promise (2 Samuel 7:29).

4. **David's prayer begins to be answered speedily**. There is a connection between the promises of 2 Samuel 7:11–16, the prayer of 2 Samuel 7:18b–29 and the events of chapter 8. When a promise is given with an oath its fulfilment is certain. Prayer for its fulfilment is likely to be speedily answered since it is prayer in God's will.

So David's kingdom begins to expand. The Philistines are subdued and cease to be a military threat (2 Samuel 8:1). Moab is defeated and two-thirds of its army is executed (8:2). In ancient times taking prisoners of war was scarcely possible and David is more lenient than other ancient generals in allowing a third of the Moabite army to go home. Zobah to the north-east (8:3–4), and their allies the Arameans (8:5–8) are defeated. Hamath in the north asks for an alliance with David (8:9–12) and Edom [1] in the south (8:13–14) is defeated. In all of this the narrator gives the honour to God (8:6, 14). The spoils of victory are not used selfishly but are dedicated to God (8:11). What is happening is that the promises of God's oath are being fulfilled. God promised to give David a great name, and it is happening (8:13). God and David are working together on a great joint-venture. **God** gives the victory wherever **David** goes.

In all of this David foreshadows Jesus. The kingdoms of this world are due to become the kingdoms of our Lord and of his Christ, and he shall reign for ever and ever (see Revelation 11:15). This is the time in the story of Israel when the territorial promise to Abraham was fulfilled. It was said that Israel should rule land from Egypt to the river Euphrates (Genesis 15:18). Now David goes out and systematically and thoroughly takes hold of everything that God had promised. Similarly God says to Jesus, *'I shall give you the nations for your inheritance'* (Psalm 2:8). Jesus is embarking on a programme of conquest. The enemies of his kingdom, unbelief, weakness in the church, sin in the world, are all destined to be conquered.

5. **David organises the practical needs of government**. As a work gets bigger it is necessary to give it structure and organisation, and David organises (2 Samuel 8:15–18) as well as prays (7:18b–29)!

David retains strong leadership himself over the organisation he is bringing into being. He takes the responsibility of seeing that right decisions and justice are provided. He avoids discrimination and sees to justice for all his people (8:15).

He has under him officials in charge of the army and in charge of a 'civil service' (8:16). The spiritual side of national life is also protected. Senior priests are available to take care of the upholding of God's worship (8:17a). Seraiah was in charge of official documents (8:17b). Benaiah took care of David's private armies, the Cherethites and Pelethites (8:18). David's sons were priests, not in the Levitical priesthood (for which as Judeans they did not qualify) but one imagines as private chaplains of some kind (8:18).

It is clear that David had great organisational abilities as well as gifts of leadership. The work of God requires a wide range of gifts. Leaders of nations and of large sections of God's work have to be people with a wide range of gifts, and a combination of spirituality, practicality, and physical strength. David's having 'entered into rest' was not a move into passivity, but a move into great blessing that gave him confidence to act with great boldness and freedom. To 'enter into rest' in connection with the promises of God sets all one's wheels in motion lubricated by the joy of knowing that victory is certain. The promises have already been inherited.

Footnote

[1] 'Aram' in 8:13 is a textual corruption for 'Edom' (see 1 Chronicles 18:12).

Chapter 16

Mephibosheth
(2 Samuel 9:1–13)

David is like God in wanting to show kindness to his enemies.
David was a man of amazing generosity. In all of his years of
struggle he had learned to forgive people and he had learned
to show only kindness to his enemies. This is what godliness
is. It is being like God, in kindness, in love towards enemies,
in generosity without gullibility or weakness.

At this point of our story David has been established in the
kingdom of all Israel for a number of years. He now wants to
show greater love than ever towards his enemies.

David's chief rival had been Saul. Saul had tried for many
years to kill David. Then after Saul's death the family of Saul
had tried to prevent David from being king. But now David is
looking for a way to be a means of blessing to his enemies.
He asks *'Is there anyone left of the house of Saul, that I may
show him kindness?'* (2 Samuel 9:1). That is what God is like.
This is what godliness is, being like God! David took the
initiative. Mephibosheth does not look for David; David
looks for him.

This is the way God feels about you! You have often
opposed God's will in your life. But God loves you anyway.

David finds a one-time employee of Saul called Ziba
(2 Samuel 9:2) and asks him about the family of Saul (9:3). It
takes a certain amount of trouble for David to be generous to
Saul's house. Most people would have felt that since the
house of Saul were no longer around they could happily be

forgotten! But David did not feel this way. He was energetically and positively looking around for a way to be good to Saul's people.

Mephibosheth is like the human race. If David is like God in his graciousness, until God intervenes in our lives we ourselves are like Mephibosheth. Mephibosheth was lame in both feet. The people of God love the weak and the despised. So does God! There is an analogy here in the way God loves us, for we were unable to walk in the ways of God. There was nothing in Mephibosheth to attract the love of David and there is nothing about us to attract God's love towards us. Why should God bother with us? *'What are human beings that you remember them? What are members of the human race that you care for them?'* (Hebrews 2:6).

With the love of God in his heart, David went to a lot of trouble to meet the needs of Mephibosheth. He found out where he was (2 Samuel 9:4), and he took the trouble to send someone to find him and bring him to the palace (2 Samuel 9:5).

1. **He did not want Mephibosheth to fear** (2 Samuel 9:6–7). One can understand why Mephibosheth should be afraid. He was from a family of enemies to David. His grandfather Saul had tried his utmost to kill David. Maybe – the thought would cross his mind – David wanted to kill him.

Most people react to God in that way. We have offended God. We have not lived for him as we ought. Maybe God is against us. We are afraid when he draws near to us. We have to learn to live on the grace of God. God is **gracious**. We are saved by his kindness. We are not saved by giving God something. We are saved by receiving something. We must learn to live without fear. God does not want us to be afraid. Our salvation is *'by grace'*.

2. **David promises that Mephibosheth will be shown kindness for Jonathan's sake** (2 Samuel 9:7). If David's kindness only had Mephibosheth in view, it might fade away and wane. Mephibosheth had nothing to attract David, and David might get weary of being kind. But since it was *'for Jonathan's sake'* it was likely to be permanent. David's love

for Jonathan was not going to change; David had sworn an oath. So God's love to us is not going to change. *'He that spared not his own Son, how shall he not with him also freely give us all things'* (Romans 8:32).

3. **David will bring restoration of lost possessions**. *'I will restore to you all the land of your father Saul'* (2 Samuel 9:7). Because of Saul, Mephibosheth has lost what could have been his. In David he will get it back. Similarly the human race was made in the image of God but lost its relationship to God. In Jesus we get back what we lost 'in Adam'. As sin once reduced us to spiritual need, now the abundance of God's grace restores what we lost (see Romans 5:19–21).

4. **Mephibosheth will have privileged access to the king's table** (2 Samuel 9:7). He would have a place of honour, a place of intimate knowledge of the affairs of the court. Similarly the Christian comes into fellowship with the Father and involvement with the concerns of the King.

5. **Mephibosheth has a provision made for his future**. In the past he has been but a *'dead dog'* (2 Samuel 9:8) but now David makes arrangements for his welfare for the rest of his life (2 Samuel 9:9). An abundance of procedures are set in motion, all intended to ensure that Mephibosheth's future is protected (2 Samuel 9:10–11).

6. **Mephibosheth is treated as a son of the king** (2 Samuel 9:11). The spiritual application is evident. We too are the sons and daughters of God with all of the privileges that involves. Mephibosheth remained under the protection of the king in Jerusalem itself where the king was never far away (2 Samuel 9:12–13).

David's great love for Mephibosheth is *'for the sake of Jonathan'*. David had sworn an oath to Jonathan who asked him not to *'cut off your loyalty from my house'* (1 Samuel 20:15, 16; 23:18; 24:21). His love for Jonathan was great. David was not intending to forget what he had promised.

The same principle is at work in the way in which God views us. We are loved with the Father's love for his Son. We are forgiven and received *'in Christ'* (Ephesians 4:32). God loves his Son and we are the people who belong to Jesus.

Chapter 17

Love Renewed and Rewarded

(2 Samuel 10:1–19)

David's amazing generosity to an enemy continues but the next time David's generosity is received with suspicion.

1. **David's love is renewed**. He had goodwill towards everyone. Once again David wants to *'show kindness'* (as in (2 Samuel 9:1). The king of a nearby territory of the Ammonites dies (10:1). David had been friendly with the father and wants to reassure his son and successor that he intends to continue in kindness and goodwill. The new king need have no fear of David (10:2a). Actually the Ammonites were not the best of neighbours. They were related to Israel and the Israelites had been commanded to treat them kindly (Deuteronomy 2:19), but they were full of animosity towards Israel. Saul had rescued a town called Jabesh-gilead from the Ammonites at an early stage of his career (1 Samuel 11:1–11; 12:12; 14:47).

David had goodwill towards everyone, even the Ammonites! There are times when he seems to act severely, but then he is implementing justice as God's king. In his personal attitudes towards people he steadily grew throughout his life in love towards everyone everywhere. David's graciousness entered into his public life. Many kings of the ancient world would have wanted to act domineeringly and harshly towards neighbouring territories, but not David!

In this David has become like God. This is what growth in holiness is. *'Be imitators of God'*, said Paul (Ephesians 5:1).

God has the same kind of goodwill towards everyone everywhere. I know there is teaching in the Bible about the way he sovereignly chooses people, but that should never make us question or query God's love and goodwill towards all men and women everywhere. God our Saviour wants all men and women to be saved (1 Timothy 2:3). He takes no pleasure in the death of a sinner (Ezekiel 18:23). He wants no one to perish (2 Peter 3:9). You do not need to have any doubts about this. God loves you! Christ died for you! David shares this characteristic of God.

2. **However David's love is rejected**. His loving ways get him into trouble. Hanun becomes suspicious of David. The suspicion was not his own, initially. Doubts were sown by the Ammonite nobles (2 Samuel 10:2b–3). It is always foolish to have a suspicious attitude towards other people, but it is even more foolish to let one's suspicions grow because of the suggestions of other people. It is a pity that Hanun did not think for himself! He actually had no reason to be suspicious of David, and even if he wanted to keep his distance from David he would have been wise to have received the ambassadors politely. But David's love was received with foolish insult (10:4) and the ambassadors were sent away half naked and with their beards foolishly disfigured.

It is part of human sinfulness that we are so often foolishly hostile towards anyone who is a rival. Everything Hanun does is ill-advised. It was reckless to reject David's kindness and loyalty to the son of an ally. It was even more foolish to respond with calculated insult. Then he goes even further in his folly. Although David found the Ammonites loathsome he did not retaliate against Hanun. He simply treats his own ambassadors with kindness and prevents them from being humiliated back in Jerusalem (10:5). They are to stay in Jericho for a while and by the time they return will not be disgraced by their half-beards. What David would have done about Hanun we do not know. For as soon as Hanun realises what he has done he takes it for granted that David will declare war, although actually David has not done that. Hanun immediately starts with preparations for battle. He persuades the Arameans to join in on his side. David's loving ways are not only rejected but seem to lead Hanun into ever deeper hostility (10:6). David's act of kindness has initiated an international conflict. He must have wished he had never shown kindness in the first place! His very kindness had got him into trouble.

He was actually being treated the same way God is treated. If David's kindliness is God-like, the response he gets is also typical of the response God gets. God's loving ways are not only ignored by the world, they are rejected with calculated insult.

Then love is replaced with wrath (2 Samuel 10:7–19). David who once had made offers of friendship towards Hanun is now about to take action against him. So too it is with God and his love. At present his Son is on offer as the channel of his love. Soon the One who is the Saviour will return as the judge. Those who rejected love will be faced with wrath. Those who rejected mercy will face justice.

3. **David's love is rewarded**. Despite his being rejected by Hanun, and despite the distresses of war, the events turn around to his advantage. At the end of the chapter the Ammonites are defeated, the Arameans are afraid to help them, and David's rest from his enemies is even more secure. David does not want war on his own territory but sees that war is inevitable. So he takes the initiative and sends Joab ahead (2 Samuel 10:7). Joab has great odds against him but he acts with skill. The Ammonites are staying near home but the Arameans are out in the open country (10:8). Joab acts with careful planning (10:9–10), with cooperation and supportiveness among the different battalions (10:11), with faith in the sovereignty of God (10:12). The cause is God's cause. Joab believes God will be with him. The Arameans were fighting as mercenaries ('hired', 2 Samuel 10:6) for cowardly people, hanging near to the gate of their town and hoping the Arameans would win the battle for them. The Israelites were fighting for God, in response to someone who had taken the initiative in aggression, under a general and king that they trusted.

The enemy armies panic (2 Samuel 10:13–14). The Arameans make a second attempt to attack (10:15–16), but David boldly takes the initiative (10:17a) and victory is his (10:17b–18). The Arameans have to make peace (10:19). So in an unexpected way David's initial kindness turned to his advantage.

Chapter 18

David and Bathsheba

(2 Samuel 11:1–4)

The Bible is remarkable for its honesty. It never makes any attempt to cover up the sins of the saints.

1. **Spiritual laziness made David vulnerable to sin**. It was a time when kings go out to battle, springtime when the weather is warmer (2 Samuel 11:1). David had been having days of great victory on the battle field. Since David's task as a king involved leading his armies into battle, his staying behind while sending out Joab and *'the whole Israelite army'* shows that he was in a period of carelessness. He had been present at previous battles (see 2 Samuel 10:17). His kingship was doing well. Yet at a time when he was doing well in military victory he was doing badly in his own life. Every able-bodied man was at war but not David! It left him vulnerable to temptation. Great men of God can fall. David was a man after God's own heart, but he was also a highly affectionate and warmhearted man. He inspired much affection in women and was scarcely ever known to have a harsh word to say to any woman. Such a man, on his own, with every able-bodied man away at war, was vulnerable to temptation.

2. **The devil is capable of arranging events to tempt us** (2 Samuel 11:2). The devil has great power, although always subject to God's control. We know (from Job chapter 1) that he can inspire raids on farms and can cause lightning to fall and houses to collapse. It is not difficult for him to manipulate events. David is doing nothing in particular and is restless. He

has been having a late-afternoon rest. He gets up and is roaming around on the roof of the palace. It so happens that Bathsheba is bathing. She is younger than David in age and is a very beautiful woman. The able-bodied men are away on the king's battles, and as she is bathing in a walled courtyard she is not being careful to avoid being seen. The king's palace was higher than most of the houses in the compound and from the top of his roof Bathsheba is visible. The idle and lonely king has a polygamous family which inevitably means that he has little companionship. He is walking around from place to place on the roof and sees his attractive neighbour. The devil can arrange temptations!

3. **Temptation has power to induce spiritual blindness**. In a moment of temptation, one can do things that in one's saner moments one would never do. David sees Bathsheba and stands there watching. He is the king, and in David's world it would be almost taken for granted that the king had absolute power. True, in Israel, things were different and kings were meant to read and obey the law of Moses. But David forgot all of this. Within no time at all his hormones were working overtime. He immediately calls a servant. *'Find out for me who is living in the house over there next to the palace'* he says, (2 Samuel 11:3). Enquiries are made. Within minutes someone in the palace has the answer. *'It is the house of Uriah, one of your best soldiers. He is away fighting for your majesty with Joab. His wife is there in the house. Her name is Bathsheba'*.

'Go and tell Bathsheba I have something I want to talk to her about', says David (2 Samuel 10:4).

Within a few minutes the beautiful Bathsheba is with David. David switches on all his charm and affectionate ways. He knows how to be charming and how to pressurise someone into doing something she did not want to do. He was not easy to resist and he was the king. Soon he had committed adultery with the wife of one of his best warriors. All his spirituality seemed to count for nothing. All his knowledge of the ways of God, all his years of seeing God answer his prayers and work powerfully in his life, everything was forgotten in those minutes when David was frantically arranging to get Bathsheba over to the palace. But this is what temptation is like. At the point where we are being tempted the devil takes us by storm; we are strangely blind.

How could the temptation have been avoided?

1. It could have been avoided if David had been more watchful about his vulnerability. *'Watch and pray so that you do not enter into temptation'* says the Scripture (Matthew 26:41). Certain situations tend to lead us into sin. Some temptation might lead one person into sin which would not lead another person into sin. Certainly times of laziness, loneliness, inactivity, avoidance of one's calling are risky times.

2. No one is ever motivated to 'watch' against situations of temptation unless his or her life is drastically and positively committed to serving God. One is not motivated to avoiding tempting situations unless one is positively and eagerly in love with God and his will and his ways. A resolution not to do this or that will be of no value whatsoever. One can make a thousand resolutions but one glimpse of a Bathsheba from a palace roof, and all such feeble resolutions will be shown up for the pathetic things that they are.

Joseph was once in a situation that was even worse (Genesis 39:12). However Joseph was so passionately and deeply committed to God and his ways, and he was keeping so far away from temptation, that he immediately fled. The secret of resisting temptation is one's **advance** commitment and level of love to God. The best approach is the indirect approach. A person in David's state is vulnerable. This is why we need to start a long way back. Watching comes even before praying. The secret of resisting temptation is to be positively rejoicing in the Lord in such a way that when the temptation comes one's joy in God is so great the temptation is resistible. The joy of the Lord is one's strength. David's neglect was to cost him dearly, and damage his reputation for the remainder of his life.

Chapter 19

When Sin is Found Out

(2 Samuel 11:5–12:13)

Many times God in his great mercy delivers us from our own foolishness. But God does not have to **block** or **counteract** our wickedness and at any time can decide to let sin reap its natural consequences, and bring its devastating results into our lives.

God arranges for David to suffer the consequences of his sin, and to be exposed. If God had not allowed disaster to overtake David, and if nothing had happened to bring David to his senses, it is likely that David would have sinned again and again in the same way. Bathsheba was a beautiful woman and a near neighbour. David was not close to God at that time. Further sin would surely have followed.

Yet God had sworn he would use and bless David. David had pleased God so much that God had sworn an oath of everlasting blessing to him. Now what will God do? When God has sworn to bless and then the one that he has sworn to bless falls into sin, God is likely to teach his child a severe lesson that will keep him from that particular sin for the rest of his days.

1. **God lets David fall into deeper sin**. Sin tends to spin a spider's web of consequences. David soon receives a note that Bathsheba is pregnant (2 Samuel 11:5). He tries three times to cover up what he has done. First, he summons Uriah home and tries to manipulate things so that the child will be thought to be Uriah's (11:6–8); it does not work (11:9). Uriah is a man with a great sense of duty and puts his concern for the soldiers above natural matrimonial pleasures

(11:10–11). Secondly, he tries to get Uriah drunk. But alcohol is not a stimulant. It is more like a tranquilliser. David's tricks do not work (11:12–13).

Soon David is desperate. He does not want it known that he could do such a despicable thing as steal the wife of one of his warriors yet what he does is even more despicable. The only thing to do if he is to prevent the secret from coming out is to marry Bathsheba and that involves arranging for the death of Uriah. So David's third resort is criminal and subject to the death penalty in the Mosaic law. Joab is instructed to arrange for Uriah's murder (2 Samuel 11:14–15). Joab arranges the matter (11:16–17). A message is sent back and in the message we learn that a number of valiant soldiers got killed at the same time (11:18–21). The message is delivered (11:22–24) and David is content (11:25). Bathsheba spent some time in mourning (11:26) and then David married her and a son was born (11:27).

2. **God lets David become hardened**. Sin has a hardening effect upon us. David committed sin with Bathsheba. It was a few hours of blinding temptation. Once the sin was committed, David perhaps regretted what he had done. Bathsheba was sent back. David's sin was an act of great wickedness and treachery. Uriah was one of David's best men. Bathsheba was the daughter of Eliab who was himself the son of David's royal counsellor Ahithophel (2 Samuel 15:12; 23:34).

But once we choose a sinful path it tends to get a grip on us and to get worse and worse. David's conscience had got hardened. Though he perhaps regretted what he had done, it was not a sufficiently powerful regret to prevent further sin. His sin of adultery led into the sin of murder. David followed the leading of sin regardless of the consequences. There was no repentance in David's life over this matter. A year went by and there was no expression of grief in David concerning what he had done. Perhaps God would not have sent Nathan if David had himself come to see what he had done. But David remained hard and unrepentant. Sin has a tendency to harden us.

3. **God exposes David's secret sin**. God had been displeased with what David had done. He let some time go by, time for David to repent. No repentance showed itself. God decided to act. God knows what we have done, and he can expose us any time he likes. It would not have been difficult for Nathan to guess what had happened. A famous warrior such as Uriah and a highly competent general such as Joab are not likely to have gone near a city wall in a time of battle (2 Samuel 11:21). Everyone knew Uriah and everyone would have wondered how David came to marry Bathsheba so swiftly. The early birth of the baby would tell Nathan everything he wanted to know. Soon he was consulting God and he was given a message for David. He tells a story of a wealthy man with an abundance of sheep and cattle, and a poor man with one animal which was more like a child to him than a farm animal. When a traveller came to the rich man, the rich man killed the precious favourite of the poor man (12:1–4).

David is angry. It was, he says, a callousness worthy of death. The law demanded fourfold compensation for crimes of theft of that nature. The essence of the rich man's sin was lack of compassion (12:5–6). Nathan replies *'You are the man'* (12:7) and proceeds to give a message from God (12:8–12). Actually everything David said about the fictional wealthy man applied to himself. His theft of Uriah's wife and the murder of Uriah were crimes worthy of death. The discipline that fell upon him was fourfold. Four people he loved died, the child that had been conceived, Amnon, Absalom and Adonijah. His lack of mercy towards Uriah was staggering. When we consider in detail the wickedness of David and his cold-blooded lack of compassion towards Uriah we are amazed – but then we are self-righteous to think we are so different.

Everything David did he did in a big way. He was guilty of big sin. But then his repentance was equally great. His restoration started at the point where he was convicted of the sinfulness of what he had done and frankly confessed it. When he said *'I have sinned'* (2 Samuel 12:13a), his recovery had started.

Chapter 20

Painful Restoration
(2 Samuel 12:7–25)

David wrote Psalm 23:3, 'He restores my soul'. Perhaps he wrote those words after his recovery from his sin in connection with Bathsheba.

1. **Nathan's message to David pointed to David's privileges** (2 Samuel 12:7b–8). David had sinned against the goodness of God. God had chosen him, empowered him, delivered him from Saul, and had been exceedingly generous to David. (*'I ... anointed ... delivered ... gave... '*). His sin was a sin against God's goodness to him.

2. **Nathan's message listed aspects of David's sin** (2 Samuel 12:9). It was despising the Word of the Lord. It was murder of a godly man. It was theft of a good man's wife. It was disgracing God's name among the Ammonites.

3. **Nathan's message told David what God's decision was concerning him** (2 Samuel 12:10–12). Violence would continue through his reign. David would suffer the treatment Uriah suffered. His wives would be stolen. Unlike Uriah he would live to see it. His family life would be devastated. The world would see what God thought about David's sin.

One reason why David was a man after God's own heart was surely his great genuineness and total honesty. David had struggled to avoid admitting his sin. But now he is as great a man in his honesty as he had been in his sin.

1. **David came to swift and thorough conviction**. He admitted totally and utterly his sin. He made no attempt to

'explain' it. He could easily have told the story of what had happened in a way that put the blame elsewhere. But *'I have sinned'* was his simple, frank, honest confession.

2. **God's forgiveness was also swift and thorough**. *'The LORD has put away your sin'*, said Nathan. *'You shall not die'*. In the law of Moses the penalty for adultery was death, but the judgement of the law is directly set aside by God (2 Samuel 12:13). Nevertheless there is a judgement. The name of God has been dishonoured. The child will die, for God will not be publicly known as approving this sin of David (2 Samuel 12:14).

3. **Conviction and forgiveness were swift but chastening was lengthy**. David was forgiven but the remainder of his life will be the story of his reaping the consequences of what he has done. Eight stories tell of the troubles that came upon him. (a) The child born to Bathsheba will die (2 Samuel 12:15–23), although a second child will be born (12:24–25) and God still gives victories to David (12:26–31). (b) Tamar suffers at the hands of Amnon (13:1–22). (c) Amnon is murdered by Absalom (13:23–39). (d) David brings his son back to Jerusalem (14:1–24), but two years go by before David will see him (14:25–33). Then Absalom shows no loyalty to David and conspires to steal the kingdom (15:1–12). (e) David is exiled from Jerusalem (15:13–16:14). (f) David's son shows immense contempt towards David (16:15–17:29). (g) Joab has to fight Absalom and kills him (18:1–33); the king goes into deep mourning (19:1–8a). (h) The Judeans receive David back (19:8b–40) but a quarrel breaks out between the Judeans and the rest of Israel (19:41–43) and it leads to a rebellion led by Sheba (20:1–25). The highlights of the stories all tell of the troubles David brought into his life by his sin.

4. **David again shows himself to be a man of godly ways**. Nathan returns to his home (12:15a), and the events that follow confirm his word. The firstborn child of David and Bathsheba becomes sick (12:15b). David starts to pray (12:16).

David prayed with great energy and passion! David did not take God's announcement as necessarily his last word. God had not sworn an oath. There was a possibility that repentance might avert the judgement of God. David prayed and prayed and prayed. He fasted. He spent seven days pleading with God. No one could distract him (2 Samuel 12:17).

But God's answer was 'no'. The child died (12:18a). At this point David ceases to pray. There are no prayers for those who have died in the Bible.

David accepts God's answer. The servants are fearful of telling him that the child has died (2 Samuel 12:18b). But David calmly accepts what has happened as God's answer (12:19–21). David explained the principle to his servants as to why he had prayed so energetically (12:22). While a situation is still 'open' one can always pray! Where no *'oath of God'* has been taken the situation is open. Even if God has given threats (as in 2 Samuel 12:14) the situation should still we regarded as open. Repentance might bring about a change. If an oath has been taken by God, no repentance is possible and no change will occur. Once a situation has closed – and death is the end-of-an-epoch – prayer and fasting will bring no change (12:23a). David is confident he will see his child again (12:23b).

It is notable that David's affection for Bathsheba and her child is very great. Many men having fathered a child in the way David did would have cared nothing more about the child. But David was a man of great love and affection and apparently truly loved this child of his. David's marriage with Bathsheba turned out to be a good one, despite its terrible beginnings. He showed affection for her child, affection for Bathsheba herself (2 Samuel 12:24–25). The marriage continued. When David was elderly it seems he still had a good marriage with Bathsheba (1 Kings 1:11–21; 28–31). Solomon, Bathsheba's first surviving child, inherited David's throne and was an ancestor of Jesus. Romans 8:28 is one of the most daring verses in the Bible. *'God works all things together for good for those who love him . . . '.* Even this awful sin was turned around and blessing came back into David's life even in connection with Bathsheba. He suffered through his sin, but God used it for good in David's life and in the story of his people. Romans 8:28 means what it says. God will forgive and restore, and will even overrule the sin that had been committed, to bring blessing, so great is his grace.

Chapter 21

Overruling Grace
(2 Samuel 12:15–31)

Eight stories tell of the troubles that came upon David after his sin. **First, the child born to Bathsheba dies** (2 Samuel 12:15–23). This will tell the world that God does not approve of what David has done. David is forgiven and his relationship to God has been restored, but he is facing severe consequences for what he has done. What should David do about his situation now that there is no way of undoing it? If the New Testament had been written, one might say he must believe Romans 8:28! He must hand the matter over to God and pick up from where he was. God knows how to give encouragements in the midst of his chastenings. David must follow the advice Samuel had given the nation once before: 'You **have** done this evil; yet do not turn away from the LORD ... The LORD will not reject his people, because the LORD was pleased to make you his own ... But be sure to fear the LORD' (1 Samuel 12:20, 22, 24). God gives David some comforts in the middle of the hard lessons he was having to learn.

1. **God overrules in his future relationship with Bathsheba**. When we confess our sins God is faithful! David starts from where he is. He never should have committed those ugly sins. But God allows him to continue from that point. He will go through sufferings and trials but God is still with him. David accepts his new wife, however bad was the start of his relationship with her. She had to live with her husband's murderer! Yet David's sincere love and affection overcame

the difficulty. So wonderful was the grace of God, his marriage to Bathsheba turned out to be a good one. He had the comfort of a wife he loved and a child he loved. He had the knowledge that Solomon was specially chosen (2 Samuel 12:24–25). David was sure that Solomon would be the heir who would sit on his throne (see 1 Chronicles 28:6, 7). He had a good relationship with Solomon. Most of David's sons seem to have thought badly of David, but Solomon spoke well of him and liked to talk of *'David my Father'* (see 1 Kings 8:15, 17, 18, 20, 24, 25, 26). Romans 8:28 was in operation before Paul thought of saying it! Bathsheba was in good relationship with David many years later (1 Kings 1:15–31).

2. **God still gives victories to David** (2 Samuel 12:26–31). The earlier oath that David would overcome the enemies around Israel had not been lost. One might expect the war against Rabbah (see 11:1) would be lost. While David was sinning with Bathsheba, Joab his general was besieging Rabbah, the chief city of the Ammonites (12:26). David was hindering the progress of the war. He himself was missing from the battle, and Joab was having to send Uriah to his death, and lose valiant men at the same time. David's staying at home was damaging the nation in more than one way. But God in his mercy does not let David's sin result in the loss of Rabbah. Joab now sends a message demanding that David get involved in the battle. He has seized Rabbah's water supply and is threatening to name the city after himself if he captures it alone (2 Samuel 12:27–28). It was a rather haughty message for a general to send to his king. Joab was not happy with David's leisure activities in Jerusalem (see (2 Samuel 11:1). He could not have been happy about having to kill Uriah (2 Samuel 11:14–21) and his estimate of David must have been lowered by the whole incident. David's relationship with Joab had been changed by his sin.

David heeded Joab and got involved in the war again. He captured Rabbah (2 Samuel 12:29) and symbolically transferred the authority of its king to himself (2 Samuel 12:30a). He plundered the city (12:30b) and imposed forced labour on his enemies (12:30b). Then the whole army, Joab's men included, returned to Jerusalem (12:30c). David and his entire army were back in Jerusalem again. He had publicly repented. God had given him victory over Rabbah.

Why does God send this mixture of chastisement and blessing upon David? If David is forgiven, why does God send further chastenings? If God is sending chastenings, is David truly forgiven?

1. **David is forgiven, but God is making it clear He does not approve of what David did**. *'You did it in secret'*, God says to David (2 Samuel 12:12), *'but I will do this thing in broad daylight'*. God is making it publicly clear that he does not approve of what David did. David is truly forgiven, but God is also expressing his view of what David had done. What David did was sin. God does not approve of it, though he has forgiven it.

2. **After a person has 'entered into rest', his sin will be more severely judged**. God had 'sworn' to bless David. Once God swears to something it cannot he withdrawn. So what does God do if someone sins who has received a covenant-oath of unconditional blessing? He cannot withdraw his promise of blessing. *'Once for ever I have sworn by my holiness, and I will not lie to David. I have sworn that his line will last for ever'* (Psalm 89:35). This was the covenant that God had given to David. It was unshakeably sure. So what does God do when such a person sins? He judges such a person even more severely. As it is said in a different connection: *'You have violated the covenant ... So I have caused you to be despised and humiliated before all the people, because you have not followed my ways'* (Malachi 2:8, 9). When God has given someone covenant-promises, and then yet further has sworn that those promises have now been obtained and cannot be lost, he is committed to his word. He is not able to withdraw his covenant, but he is able to deal most severely with sins against his grace. David had 'entered into rest'. He had secured the covenant-promises in a way that could not be lost. When he sinned God did not withdraw the kingdom; he had already given his oath. Instead he expressed his displeasure in a mixture of chastenings and encouragements.

Chapter 22

Reaping Corruption
(2 Samuel 13:1–39)

In **this** life, *'he who sows to please the flesh will back from the flesh reap corruption'* (Galatians 6:8). Eight stories tell of the troubles that came upon David after his sin.

In a second incident, Tamar suffers at the hands of Amnon (2 Samuel 13:1–22). David's sin was repeated in the life of Amnon. There was a changed relationship with his sons. He never had disciplined them. Perhaps he wanted to guide them by love alone. But David's sin took away any respect they had for him. The greatest man of all Old Testament history, the man 'after God's own heart', had no respect from his sons. Soon what David had done was to repeat itself in the life of Amnon. David had fallen impetuously in love with Bathsheba and had eventually got his way. David's sons now know that Bathsheba is David's favourite and his new queen. In due course Bathsheba's eldest surviving son would be the king. David lost the respect of his sons during this time. Judging by David's great grief over Absalom when he died later, David experienced great personal tragedy through these events, for David loved his sons dearly.

The life of David's daughter Tamar was ruined. As David had fallen impetuously in love with Bathsheba, so now his oldest son Amnon falls in love with his half-sister Tamar. David had got his Bathsheba; Amnon wants Tamar. If David could use his power as king to do what he liked, Amnon now wanted to use his power as prince and have Tamar. David's sin was a temporary lapse and he recovered. But it gave rise to Amnon's sin and Amnon never recovered.

Amnon became infatuated with the beautiful Tamar (2 Samuel 13:1–2), and there are always those around who will help us into the pathways of sin. Amnon has a 'friend', David's nephew Jonadab, who is ready to suggest a wicked plan (2 Samuel 13:3–5).

All of David's sins seem to be repeating themselves only in an even worse form. David sent for Bathsheba; Amnon succeeds in bringing Tamar to him by an even more deceitful trick (2 Samuel 13:6–8). David imposed his will on Bathsheba; Amnon forces Tamar. David had no compassion on Uriah; Amnon has no compassion on Tamar (13:9–14). Amnon's wickedness was more cruel than anything David had done to Bathsheba, and yet Amnon was in a position to say *'If my father could take whatever he wanted, why cannot I?'* David was repentant but Amnon never was. David stayed loving and gracious and loyal to Bathsheba for the rest of his life. Amnon's 'love' turned instantly to hate, the moment his sin was finished (13:15). Having ruined her life, he now refused to have anything to do with her (13:16–18a). Amnon copied the worst in David, but he never copied the best in David. Soon what has happened becomes obvious (13:18b–19). Absalom finds out what has happened and shortly is nursing murderous hatred for his half-brother Amnon (13:20–22).

Eventually, there is a third repercussion of the sin of David: Amnon is murdered by Absalom (2 Samuel 13:23–35).

Absalom kept his hatred secret for two years, allowing time for Amnon to become careless. If Amnon could craftily scheme to get his half-sister, Absalom could craftily scheme to kill his half-brother. David allowed himself to be tricked by Amnon, but now was tricked by Absalom (13:23–27). Yet still God's faithfulness to David continued, for God protected David. He too had been invited to the festival! Absalom wanted to kill David for his part in what had happened. At Absalom's command Amnon was killed; the rest of the king's sons fled since it seemed they were due to be killed also (13:28–29). The news came to David that all his sons had been killed; he suffered agonies of grief (13:30–31).

He was not in a position to say a word. His own behaviour had been too similar. David had 'entered into rest' yet now was 'reaping corruption'. The promise there would be an eternal 'Son of David' was unshakeably sure. This is all the more reason why God has to deal very severely with David. David's sin will not affect the progress of God's purpose to send Jesus as the 'Son of David'. Yet God wants it to be unmistakably clear to everyone. Sin does not pay. God overruled in the case of David and Bathsheba and yet David had trials and troubles all of the rest of his life that stemmed from his sin. He had been sowing to please the flesh; now he will reap back from the flesh corruption in his kingdom for the remainder of his life.

The initial news that reached David about the slaughter of his family proved to be exaggerated. He is comforted by a flatterer. Jonadab, who had given ugly advice to Amnon about how to get his sister, now has a comforting word for David (2 Samuel 13:32–35)! There are always people wanting to flatter a royal family or any other kind of powerful leadership. Their motive is to get themselves to a position of prestige and advantage for themselves. They want people of importance to promote them and so they will flatter anyone. Jonadab had inside knowledge about Absalom's intentions. So why had he not warned David before? Why had he not warned his 'friend' Amnon? Now he is glad to seem to be important by being able to give welcome information to David. But all of his professed friendship is deceitful.

David's family were in great distress in all of this (2 Samuel 13:36). Absalom went into exile with his mother's father, Talmai, who was king of a small country called Geshur (13:37; see 3:3). David grieved first over his son Amnon, and then spent three years of painful distress concerning Absalom (13:38–39).

One has to feel sorry for David! He is reaping what he had sown. He had never disciplined his sons. He had disfigured his reputation with them. Then he had refused to do anything about Amnon. The result is deep suffering. David was 'reaping corruption'.

Chapter 23

Deception

(2 Samuel 14:1–24)

Now a fourth stage in these calamities develops. David experiences deception and betrayal by his son. He had betrayed Uriah. Now he himself will learn through his own son what it feels like to be betrayed. Absalom shows no loyalty to David and conspires to steal the kingdom.

It begins with a piece of deception by a clever lady. Joab was a soldier and political leader before he was anything else. He knows of David's longing for Absalom (2 Samuel 14:1), and thinks that it will be of no value to the nation for Absalom to be in exile. So three years after the murder of Amnon he makes plans to get Absalom back into the favour of David. Absalom was the oldest son of David and one might think next in line for the throne. But Amnon is dead and Kileab, David's second son via Abigail, has died or lacks ambition. Joab is helping the third son, the man who is likely to be the next king. Joab sends for a 'wise', that is, a 'clever' woman. She pretends she had two sons. One of the sons – so the story goes – killed the other (14:2–6). The story is an imitation of what happened with David, Amnon and Absalom. Now – so the story goes – the second son is lost to her also because his life is in danger (14:7).

David wishes to dismiss this case speedily and gives vague promises to help (*'I will issue an order'*, 14:8). But the woman wants something more definite before she is going to reveal what she has really come to say. She is so confident, she suggests, in the justice of her cause that she will invite the judgement upon herself and her family if there is any miscarriage of justice (14:9). So the king goes a step further. He promises that if anyone troubles the lady, the troublemaker can be referred to him and the king will deal with it (14:10). But the woman is still not satisfied, and asks for a greater assurance. She asks for an oath (*Let the king call upon the LORD his God'*) that will totally commit the king and will ensure that the threat of violence against her son is totally stopped (2 Samuel 14:11a). At that point the woman gets what she wants. David gives an oath (*'as surely as the LORD lives'*), and assures her that her son will be totally protected no matter what he has done (2 Samuel 14:11b). David gave a promise in verse 8 (*'I will issue an order on your behalf'*). But a promise might be left aside; an oath is a legally obligatory matter and cannot be left aside. David might change his mind about a promise. He will never change his mind about an oath.

The clever woman from Tekoa now gets David to face the logic of what he has just said. He has been willing to intervene with mercy in the case of a son who murdered his brother, and to give a solemn promise bound by an oath. Why will he not apply the same mercy to his own son? What he is currently doing is *'against the people of God'* (2 Samuel 14:12–13a). The entire nation is suffering (she suggests) because David will not show mercy to his son (14:13b). Amnon has died and his death cannot be reversed; we all have to die sometime (14:14a). Meanwhile, she says, God loves to be gracious and bring back banished ones to himself (14:14b). Why does not David do the same?

In verse 15 she reverts back to her original story. Verses 12–14 have been a pretended digression – though they are the real burden of what the woman has come to say. She fears her family will kill her second son and has come to the king for help (2 Samuel 14:15). She again asks David to intervene in protection of her son. If an avenger kills her son, not only will the son be killed, she too as a widow will lose her inheritance, the family land (14:16). She pleads with the king to give her a favourable reply (14:17a) and flatters him; he is like an angel in his wisdom (14:17b).

At this point the clever lady has gone too far. David recognizes Joab's work in all of this (2 Samuel 14:18–19a). She admits he is right but repeats her flattery (14:19b–20). Her trick succeeds and David allows Absalom back (14:21–24).

There is one great lesson from this story. **A man still living with a guilty past is likely to make major errors of judgement**. One part of the sin of men and women is that *'their tongues practise deceit'* (Romans 3:13). We are constantly warned 'Don't be deceived' (James 1:16 & 22). The woman of Tekoa is clever and convincing. But it has Joab's worldly wisdom behind it. He is supporting Absalom for the sake of his position when David is succeeded in the kingship by his oldest surviving son (as Joab thinks). It is misleading talk. There is nothing godly about it. It is weakness for David to give way. He should have acted justly in dealing with Amnon but could not bring himself to condemn his son. Now he should be at least keeping his son Absalom in exile, or securing just punishment for the murder of Amnon. But David does none of these things. He is paralysed by the feeling that it was all his fault. He is quite unable to exercise justice in dealing with his sons. He is enticed into releasing the woman's fictional second son – against the Mosaic law – and so has been tricked into bringing back someone who is a known murderer into Jerusalem. He deceived Uriah; now he is deceived himself.

The way to steer away from deception is to have a clear conscience, to be in good fellowship with God through the blood of Jesus, to regularly seek his guidance. David is haunted by what had led to the sins of his sons – the Bathsheba incident – and so is deceived. Only in closeness to Jesus is there safety from deception.

Chapter 24

Betrayal

(2 Samuel 14:25–15:12)

This section of 2 Samuel is telling in detail the sad story of the consequences of David's sin. The child born to Bathsheba has died. Tamar had suffered at the hands of Amnon. Amnon has been murdered by Absalom. We are still in what I have called the fourth stage in these calamities. David experiences incredible betrayal by his son. David brings his son back to Jerusalem (2 Samuel 14:1–24). In this a mistake has been made. David has been deceived.

Absalom is arrogant, self-willed, and has no interest in his father's well-being. David longed for Absalom, but Absalom never longed for David. He was good looking (14:25) and proud of his thick and abundant hair (14:26). He had loved his sister Tamar and named his daughter after her (14:27). But he had allowed his bitterness over Tamar's being molested to bring wickedness into his life. David has been persuaded to bring Absalom back to Jerusalem but two years have gone by and David still refuses to see him. After two years Absalom asks to see Joab (14:28–29) and when he gets no answer takes stronger action to force Joab to see him (14:30–31). He sets fire to Joab's barley field and gets his attention rapidly. Then when Joab comes he forcefully requests to see David himself (14:32). Joab speaks for him and Absalom is received by David (14:33).

But soon the folly of what David and Absalom had done becomes apparent. Absalom rebels (15:1–12). Joab had brought back Absalom by the deceptive trickery of the woman of Tekoa. Now worldly wisdom is being proved a failure.

The work of God can suffer attack in different ways. The church of Jesus can suffer from persecution or from internal division or from deception and error. Here in the wickedness of Absalom we see an account of how deception can take place.

1. **Absalom began by play-acting and pretentiousness** (2 Samuel 15:1). He acted the part of a typical ancient king, with power and influence, and gathered around him the status symbols of horses and a personal escort of fifty men. He acted as if he were the next king.

2. **He undermined confidence in David** (2 Samuel 15:2–4). He prevented people bringing their grievances to David (15:2) by getting to them before they reach the city-gate where courts of justice were held (15:2a). He would make use of the desires of each tribe and would suggest that a man from such-and-such a town or from this particular tribe would not get justice from David (15:2b–3), since he had no officials who would uphold justice. It was a way of quietly undermining the popularity of David, and of promoting himself as the hope for justice in the land (2 Samuel 15:4).

3. **He pretended to a love of the people which was not genuine** (2 Samuel 15:5). People can be extraordinarily gullible. Absalom's past record revealed that he was a cunning and clever murderer but the people were willing to view him as a champion of justice. Within a short time he had stolen the hearts of the people (15:6).

4. **When he had prepared the way he stole the kingdom from David** (2 Samuel 15:7–12). Soon he found an occasion to go to Hebron, which had been the king's capital before Jerusalem was made the capital. From there he sent messengers to proclaim that he was king throughout the country (15:10). At the same time he invited many guests from Jerusalem to be with him in Hebron. They did not know what they were being invited to. It gave the impression of his having a large quantity of important supporters from Jerusalem (15:11).

He persuaded Ahithophel to join him (15:12). Ahithophel was an important counsellor of the king, and an eminent person. Absalom was fortunate in getting a person from Jerusalem as important as he was. But one can understand why Ahithophel would be willing to join in a campaign against David. He was Bathsheba's grandfather (2 Samuel 11:3; 23:34) and had reason to hold a grudge against David. Absalom's rebellion is one of a number of ways in which David is made to feel the pain of betrayal. He had treated Absalom with generosity, allowing him a place in the life of Jerusalem. But Absalom's entire life had been a pretence. His only interest is to become the king. David himself had cruelly betrayed Uriah, sending him back into battle carrying in his hand the instruction that he himself should be killed. Uriah went to Joab carrying his own sentence of death. David had betrayed one of his greatest men. It was wickedness on David's part. But now David is receiving from the hand of his own son the same kind of treatment that he himself had given Uriah. If he thinks Absalom is wicked it would not be a big step to remember that he had once done something similar. God can teach us lessons in life by getting us to experience from someone else the very treatment that we have been giving others.

If we are betrayed we recall it was something that Jesus experienced. His closest friends abandoned him when he was arrested. In David's case, his being betrayed was part of the Father's teaching him how wicked he had been to betray Uriah to his death. In Jesus' case it was part of what was needed for him to become a perfect Saviour. Jesus had to go through some of the painful experiences we go through in order to convince us that he is truly sympathetic. David's son betrayed him. One day a Son of David would make up for what this son of David did. One day Jesus the Son of David would be utterly loyal to his Father. Absalom son of David wishes to remove his father and take over his father's kingdom. Cruel and deceitful betrayal was the means he chose to that end.

One day Jesus, God's Son of David would do the opposite.

One day Jesus would come delighting to do the will of his Father, and upholding and furthering the kingdom of his Father.

Chapter 25

Exile

(2 Samuel 15:13–16:14)

We are still following the way in which the prophecy of Nathan works out in David's life. *'I will raise up calamity against you from your own household'* said God (2 Samuel 12:11). First David's child dies. Then Tamar is molested. Amnon is murdered. Absalom rises against his father.

Now a fifth repercussion of the sin of David develops: David is exiled from Jerusalem (2 Samuel 15:13–16:14). This is the most startling of all. Jerusalem was the place in which all the hopes of David were centred. He had received an oath from God that his son would build a temple there. David thought he knew that the child who would build the temple would be Solomon. Now the greatest promises he had ever received seem to be threatened. Is he to lose his kingship and be exiled from Jerusalem?

Absalom had prepared the way for several years. David was told *'The hearts of the people of Israel are with Absalom'* (2 Samuel 15:13). Things looked bad for David. Absalom is unscrupulous and a proven killer and David's life is in danger from his own son. When he was on the palace roof in Jerusalem, arranging for Bathsheba to come to him, he did not imagine that one day he would be exiled from that very city because of the sin he was walking into.

But David is not overwhelmed with panic. He had *'entered into rest'* with regard to the promises of God concerning his future. Absalom was not the one through whom the promises would go forward. David is still totally assured about the promises of God. God's oath to the Davidic dynasty is sure

(Psalm 89:19–37). Not even serious sin will make God change His mind. Although David cannot entirely predict the future, he has strong hope that Jerusalem and his kingdom will come back to him. He is still a skilful soldier and much more experienced in war than Absalom. He wants to save the city (2 Samuel 15:14) and he needs time to get his army together.

Again amidst the chastenings of God there are strong encouragements. He finds out who his real supporters are. **The opportunity for expressing faith in David is there for those who believe in him**. His palace staff are loyal to him (2 Samuel 15:15). He himself has faith in God's promises, and is sufficiently confident in coming back that he leaves ten concubines to care for the palace (15:16). He and his supporters pause at 'the Far House' (as the Hebrew means) on the edge of the city and David reviews his regiments of soldiers (15:17). He offers Ittai an opportunity to go back to safety with 'king' Absalom (15:18–20) but Ittai pledges himself to loyalty to David (15:21) and David is glad to have him (15:22).

There were others who were intensely loyal to him. Large numbers of the local population express their support for David and leave the city with him (2 Samuel 15:23). The two senior priests Zadok and Abiathar support him, but David sends them and their sons back to Jerusalem with instructions that they keep him informed (15:24–29). It was a time of great crushing humiliation for David. He appeared to be losing his kingship, his ministry, his reputation as a soldier. It seemed cowardly to be fleeing the capital. David was weeping with emotion. The people were in distress (15:30).

It was like the time of Jesus on the cross. Appearances looked grim. Yet such a time reveals who has faith and who does not. Ittai believed David was God's man. *'Wherever my lord the king may be, whether it means life or death, there will your servant be'* (2 Samuel 15:21).

On the other hand some have deserted him, having no faith in him. Ahithophel, David's royal counsellor, has joined Absalom. David prays his advice will be overthrown (2 Samuel 15:31) and sends Hushai the Arkite to frustrate Ahithophel's advice (2 Samuel 15:32–37). There are also people who want to exploit the situation to their own advantage. Ziba has seen David's generosity and wants some of Mephibosheth's advantages that have come from David's plenty (2 Samuel 16:1–4). His tale is deceitful.

David faces also the curses of Shimei (2 Samuel 16:5–14). He faces the condemnation of Shimei with calmness. He knows that what is happening to him is all part of God's instruction to him, part of his needed adversity after his carelessness at the time of the Bathsheba incident. So it is possible that God has lessons for him to learn even from the resentment of Shimei.

All of this is a picture of Jesus on the cross. Jesus is a king but is often rejected by the world. His position is capable of misinterpretation. That was David's position. But it is in such a situation that faith or unbelief reveal themselves. Ahithophel had seemed to be a close friend but he was Bathsheba's grandfather and he had the heart of a traitor and betrayer. It is only when our position is insecure and success uncertain that the true convictions of men and women about us surface. Shimei curses David because he thinks that David's cause is lost. Ittai adheres to David because he is convinced David is God's king.

It is a situation of uncertain interpretation that appears when we see our Lord Jesus as the one who was crucified. The eyes of faith see him as God's king but it was a time of humiliation for him. David was being humiliated for his own sins; Jesus was humiliated for our sins.

Faith is seeing **now** what everyone will see **soon**. In a few days it would be obvious that David would be returned to power. Ittai would be raised to honour and influence. Shimei would be reduced to grovelling shame. But at the moment none of that is apparent. What determines how people relate to David is what their faith is concerning his future. Our faith concerning Jesus' future is that every knee will bow to him, every tongue will confess that he is Lord. He is king **now** but not everyone knows it. We believe it now! We bow the knee before him now! Our tongues confess that he is king now!

Chapter 26

Protection in Dark Days
(2 Samuel 16:15–17:29)

The chastenings of David move into a further stage. **The sixth of eight stories of disaster tells of a time when David's own son shows immense contempt towards David** (2 Samuel 16:15–17:29). There are four characters in this story: Hushai, Absalom, Ahithophel and David.

1. **Hushai is in a compromising situation**. He pretends to be a supporter of Absalom. Absalom arrives in Jerusalem (2 Samuel 16:15). Hushai greets him. *'Long live the king!'* he says (16:16) but he does not say which one! When Absalom is suspicious (16:17), he has an answer *'The one chosen by the Lord . . . I will remain with him!'* (16:18). Again it is capable of more than one interpretation; it could refer to David! But Hushai cannot keep up the double-talk and soon his evasion turns to ugly deception (16:19). We cannot judge him harshly. Israel, the people of God, was a worldly nation. Warfare was not *'spiritual warfare'*! 2 Corinthians 10:4a was not always true for them. The weapons of **their** warfare were often carnal.

We tolerate Hushai because of the circumstances he was in. But for ourselves the requirement is *'Do not put on the outward front of being conformed to this world . . .'* (Romans 12:2).

2. **Absalom is pushed a step further into resolute sin**. He is persuaded by Ahithophel to take his father's concubines (2 Samuel 16:20–22). Ahithophel's advice is famous

(2 Samuel 16:23), and is deadly in its likelihood of success. The purpose of the suggestion is to force Absalom and his supporters to the point of no return in their rebellion. Once Absalom has done such a thing it will be so offensive that there will be no possibility of easy reconciliation with his father David. Ahithophel is determined to get Absalom to the point where he cannot easily go back to his father and bring the rebellion to an end.

It is typical of the ways of Satan. He will gladly push us into some piece of folly and persuade us to be so committed to the ways of sin that it seems impossible for any return to be made. The last thing he wants is any way back out of wickedness. If he can shut off the routes to repentance, he will.

Absalom is deceived by his own pride. Ahithophel's first piece of advice is taken. Then he has a second word of advice (2 Samuel 17:1–3). He proposes to take twelve thousand men and catch up with David in a few hours. He will aim at killing no one except the king. A bloodless revolution will be easier to handle than a civil war. The plan seems good to everyone (17:4). But God is capable of bringing even the cleverest schemes of wickedness to nothing. God can overthrow the wisdom of the wise. Ahithophel was not remembering the way God had delivered David from Goliath and from years of threats from Saul. Hushai is given a chance to put forward different advice (17:5–6). God gives him what to say. Ahithophel's advice, Hushai says, is not good *'this time'*. Tactfully, he suggests that it has been quite good before (17:7). He stresses the heroism of David's men. He is playing on Absalom's insecurity and fear. He stresses David's experience (17:8) and the likelihood that he is well hidden (17:9a). David is capable of making a speedy attack, and then the rumour might get around that Absalom's troops have been slaughtered. He is playing on Absalom's concern for his reputation (17:9b). Such slaughter would spread terror throughout the land (17:10). Hushai's advice is: Absalom must summon the whole of Israel and lead the army against David himself (17:11). He paints a glorious picture of Absalom leading the army into great victory. If need be, they will drag the entire city into the valley (17:12–13)!

It is the last point that gets Absalom to change his mind. Absalom is a vain and proud person, used to flattery and accustomed to admiring himself (see 14:25–26). The idea that he, not Ahithophel, will lead an army against David appeals to him. Ahithophel's plan is dropped.

Sin has a habit of defeating itself. The very sin that had been steadily growing in Absalom's life is the sin that leads him into faulty judgements and brings about his downfall.

3. **Ahithophel is also deceived by his own pride**. He is famous for his wisdom. He has been regarded as if he were as good as God for giving advice (2 Samuel 16:23). Now suddenly there comes a humiliating blow to his pride. *'The advice of Hushai is better'* (17:14). God is again letting sin defeat itself.

Hushai is able to tell the two priests what has happened (17:15) and to get David to safety (17:16). The two sons of the two priests receive a message through a servant girl (17:17) but a follower of Absalom observes the young men hanging around En-Rogel some way outside Jerusalem (17:18). The young men move further away to Bahurim and hide (17:18b–19). When Absalom sends soldiers to investigate they fail to find anything incriminating (17:20). Later the two men get to David and he acts on their word (17:21–22). God is at work in protecting the cause of his king. God is allowing David to be very severely chastened. There was once a time when he failed to go out to battle (11:1–2). God is chastising him by forcing him to be amidst terrible conflict. Yet at the same time God is protecting his servant. God knows how to chastise and to protect at the same time.

But the humiliation of Ahithophel is more than he can bear. He is the Judas of the Old Testament. His betrayal of David brought him no blessing. He committed suicide (17:23–24). He would rather die than be humiliated by another being preferred to him. This famous 'wise man' was not so wise after all.

4. **David has to endure, seek God's help and wait**. He is

being severely chastened and is in exile from all his blessings and comforts. But it will not go on for ever. In the midst of these dark days God is still with him. Support came that made life bearable, even amidst the chastening of God (17:27–29).

Chapter 27

A Tender-Hearted Father

(2 Samuel 18:1–18)

In the seventh of the stories we are considering, Joab has to fight Absalom and kills him (2 Samuel 18:1–33) and David goes into deep mourning (19:1–8a). We recall that God said to David *'I will raise up calamity against you from your own household'* (2 Samuel 12:11).

1. **David is being forced to face what he had done to Uriah**. Chastening often takes the form of something that makes us face what we have done. It is agonising for David. He organises his army (2 Samuel 18:1–2a) but the army he is organising is about to go out after his son. David had sent Uriah to his death at the hands of an enemy army. Now David is being made to face the reality of what this means. His own son is now facing the possibility of death at the hands of David's army.

The officers persuade David to remain behind (2 Samuel 18:2b–4). Normally his soldiers would have wanted him to be with them (see 1 Samuel 8:20) and that was his usual practice. 2 Samuel 11:1–2 records an unfortunate exception. But now they do not feel he should be with them in a time when they are hunting David's own son. They are sparing his feelings. Also it is likely that David might not have his usual good judgement on the battle field. He is as much concerned to keep his son safe as to win the battle. He is acting more as a father than as a king. Yet this is the very thing he should have done to Uriah. He should have been a father to Uriah, protecting his general who was loyal to him.

2. **David reflects the heart of God in his incredible generosity**. Despite the great wickedness of Absalom, despite even the shocking treatment of David's concubines, despite the deliberate attempt to kill him, David still wanted to protect Absalom. No wonder David is a man after God's own heart. The people hear David urging his three generals not to kill Absalom (2 Samuel 18:5–6). Despite all that has happened David is still affectionate and tolerant towards his son. In the story of David it has become apparent that David was a very warm-hearted and affectionate man. His soldiers loved him. Women admired him. He himself had great affection for his sons. Yet his great affection sometimes led him astray. His love for Bathsheba was passionately self-centred and brought him trouble. His love for his sons was such that he never disciplined them. This is understandable. They each had different mothers and in a polygamous family David would not have been close to their mothers. The scandal of his taking Bathsheba led them into disloyalty and now David is suffering the agony of losing a son he loves.

David's love was full of impurities. God's love is parallel but is without weakness or impurity. This is an encouragement for us. If David had a very great loving nature and a passionate desire to be generous and forgiving, how much more shall we find God to be altogether good to us. It is this tenderness of character in David that God loved. But in this we see God himself. If David went to such extraordinary lengths to protect a wayward son we must see in him something of the extraordinary lengths God will go to, to hold on to us and protect us from the folly of our own ways.

3. **Absalom's pride receives its eventual judgement**. God is chastening David but God has not abandoned him and the promises concerning David's royal line cannot be aborted. A battle in the forest of Ephraim takes place (2 Samuel 18:6–8). It was an area of rough country and dense forest. More were killed by the nature of the terrain than were killed in the fighting. It was full of pits, precipices and pools. To try to run for

safety in thick forest was itself dangerous, as Absalom's story illustrates.

Absalom himself is caught (18:9). The story does not mention his hair, but we evidently are meant to remember 1 Samuel 14:26. He had been proud of his hair but it could not have helped him when he was caught in the branches of a tree. His plight was soon told to Joab (2 Samuel 18:10). The man who discovered Absalom would not kill him and so disobey what he knew was the king's will (18:11–13). But Joab was a tough military general and had no scruples. The needs of the country came above David's personal feelings for his son. Joab and his men killed Absalom (18:14–15), the pursuit was called off (18:16) and Absalom was buried (18:17).

At this point the storyteller presses home the lesson of the narrative. He mentions an event which showed Absalom's vanity (18:19). His three sons (see 14:27) had apparently died while they were young. Absalom's concern was to be famous. He erected a 'pillar' because he wanted something visible and permanent that would cause him to be remembered.

It is another indication of how much, deep within, we desire to receive glory. Man was created in glory. He was to be for a little while lower than the angels and was then to get to be crowned with glory and honour as a reward for having lived for God. But man sinned, and today *'lacks the glory of God'* (Romans 3:23). Yet he always hungers for glory and wants to get back what he has lost. The only true way to get glory is to receive it from the hands of God as a reward for having lived for Him. God's final judgement of mercy for the godly is that we *'receive a name'* for ever and ever, for having served God. Jesus says *'I will not erase his name ... I will confess his name'* (Revelation 3:5). The alternative is *'disgrace and everlasting contempt'* (Daniel 12:2).

Absalom wanted a memorial commemorating his endeavours, but he received a memorial commemorating his wickedness. He chose a route which led to a pile of stones, speaking of failure, death and shame, instead of a returning to the everlasting forgiveness of a tender-hearted father.

Chapter 28

Good News and Bad News

(2 Samuel 18:19–19:8a)

The news of Absalom's death is sent to David (2 Samuel 18:19–32). David is shattered by the news (18:33).

Zadok's son wants to tell David the news of Absalom's death (18:19) but Joab discourages him (18:20). Someone else is sent (18:21) but Ahimaaz insists on going also (18:22–23). Ahimaaz believes this is good and wonderful news. The country is saved for David. He wants to be the bearer of good news.

David himself is eager for good news and cannot bear the thought that he is about to hear the news of tragedy. When something is exceedingly painful we are inclined to shut our minds off from the truth. David says that it will be good news if a runner is coming alone but bad news if there is more than one. As it happens there is more than one runner so that ought to tell him that the news will not be good. David cannot bear the thought that there is bad news on the way concerning Absalom and persuades himself that the news is good (18:24–27).

Ahimaaz is young and does not have the sympathy needed to see things from David's viewpoint. For him the news is entirely good. The kingdom has been preserved for David. *'All is well!'* he says. *'Blessed is the LORD your God who has delivered up to punishment the men who rebelled against my lord the king'* (18:28).

David is not interested in such pious talk. All he wants to know is *'Is it well with the young man Absalom?'* (18:29).

Ahimaaz will not give a straight answer to that question and says *'I saw some great excitement, but I did not know what it was'*. What is the good of a messenger who will not tell you what you want to know? David must have been exasperated. Why will the young man not tell him the one thing he wants to discover?

He tells Ahimaaz to wait and turns to the Cushite (2 Samuel 18:30–32a). He is determined to get the answer to the one thing he wants to find out. At last he finds out what he is desperate to know. Even the Cushite will not talk straight but he at least says enough for David to know the answer. Absalom is dead (18:32b). The king is shattered. He had been hoping against hope that somehow Absalom would survive and David would forgive him and have him back. He is utterly crushed and brokenhearted (18:33).

Truth is more important than our own prominence. Ahimaaz wants to be a messenger but is not concerned to tell the total truth to David. He simply wants to get the glory for being the messenger who announces David's victory. Yet he is not a very faithful messenger because he is more concerned about the glory he will get through the message than he is about telling the truth and the whole truth.

The gospel message of Jesus is good news first and foremost. It tells us of the answer to our plight at the same time that it tells us what that plight is. Although tact and wisdom are needed there is to be no question of avoiding the message: we have renounced clever ways of presenting the truth. We openly state what the truth is and hope that it will commend itself to every person's conscience (2 Corinthians 4:2).

Affection is wonderful but it has to be affection in God. David is the most tender-hearted and affectionate man in the Bible. His soldiers loved him. They knew he could not fight against his own son and persuaded him to keep out of what had to be done. Women admired David, as the stories of Michal and Abigail and Bathsheba make plain. He himself had great affection for his sons.

Great affection is a wonderful thing. It binds friends and relatives together. It can lead to companionship and warmth.

There is no greater earthly blessing. This is what the human race was made for, to be a people bound together in love under God.

Yet great affection has to be subordinated to God and kept within the bounds of the will of God. David's great affection sometimes led him astray. At this point it is affecting his judgement. We have seen his love for Bathsheba was self-centred and brought him trouble. His love for his sons was without good judgement. Also the scandal of his killing Uriah led them into disloyalty and now David is suffering the agony of losing a son he loved (18:33).

Good advice may come from someone one does not like. David's mourning for Absalom was soon seen by Joab to be excessive (2 Samuel 19:1–6) and he rebukes David. David never ceased to love even a son who had betrayed him. Joab was not the kind of person to have much sympathy for that. Yet Joab's judgement is right. Sometimes cool calm detachment is more helpful than deep involvement. Joab is a brutal and callous man. Yet his calm advice is actually correct.

David did not like Joab. Through his entire kingship Joab had the kind of power where he could do terrible things and escape the penalty for it. Yet sometimes those who are our enemies can see things in a way we cannot. Enemies and critics have a habit of picking on our weak points. When someone we do not get on well with is observing us, they do not focus on our strong points. Rather they focus on our weak points. Although their motives for saying what they do may not always be good, they might be right,

Joab was right. David needed to take action to regain the kingdom. Life has to go on, even amidst painful bereavement. David is a king as well as a father. David has the intelligence to see that Joab is right. He takes Joab's advice (2 Samuel 19:7–8a) and starts on the task of regaining and reuniting his kingdom.

Chapter 29

A Worthy King

(2 Samuel 19:8b–40)

The stories we are considering are not seeking to relate every detail of the life of David. There are many projects that David achieved which are not mentioned in 1–2 Samuel at all. There are records of some of them in 1 Chronicles. What the narrator is doing here is giving an account of the many disastrous consequences of David's sin, in connection with Uriah and Bathsheba.

Now comes the eighth of these stories: the Judeans receive David back (2 Samuel 19:8b-40) **but a quarrel breaks out between the Judeans and the rest of Israel** (19:41–43) **and it leads to a rebellion led by Sheba** (20:1–25).

Sometimes we make a bad mistake and then wish we could change our minds. This was the way it was in Israel immediately after the death of Absalom.

1. **The people had made a bad mistake**. A bad decision had been made when they had allowed themselves to be enticed away from David. Absalom had pretended to love the people but he was a proud man and desired only glory for himself, not the privilege of protecting God's people. Now the people of 'Israel' (the northern part of the country as opposed to Judah in the south) realise how foolish they have been. The people were having second thoughts about David (2 Samuel 19:8b). Their decision had not been blessed in any way at all. They had lost the one who had delivered them (19:9) in days

99

gone by. Absalom whom they had favoured had proved a failure (19:10).

Having made a bad mistake, they begin to blame each other. They point out to each other that what they did was wrong and all ask each other *'Why do you not bring the king back?'* They were apparently all leaving it to each other to take action and as a result no one was taking action.

Have you ever made a bad mistake and then been paralysed when you realise what you have done? You tend to blame others and hope that others will do something. You wish you could somehow come back to where you were before but it seems that nothing can be done.

2. **David takes the initiative in bringing the rebels back to himself**. A bad mistake does not mean that David can never be the king again. David is often like Jesus. He is like Jesus here in that while the rebels are wondering about bringing the king back to be the lord over their lives, the king himself takes action. This is like Jesus. When we are only beginning to think about undoing what we have done, he is already a step ahead of us and is coming towards us before we are coming towards him.

Instructions are sent to Abiathar and Zadok. They must suggest to the elders of Judah (the south, not the north) that they too should take steps to bring David back as king (19:11–12). David is after all a Judean.

3. **David does something that lets everyone know that even the greatest of rebels will receive forgiveness**. Amasa is to replace Joab as general of the nation's forces (19:13). He had commanded Absalom's forces. David's announcement makes it clear that there is forgiveness for the worst of offenders. No doubt there are other reasons also in David's mind. He is not happy about having as general one who has so persistently shown himself to be a killer, without regard for David's will. The killing of Absalom was something David was not willing to overlook. We shall discover Joab is not so easy to put down. For the moment, however, David's invitation to Amasa makes public his willingness to be generous in forgiveness.

So generous is David in his warmth towards Israel, the

entire people of Judah want the king to return. He wins their heart (19:14a). The men of Judah, plus many Benjamites including Shimei and Ziba come to welcome him (19:14b–18a).

Another rebel who receives forgiveness is Shimei, who had cursed David when he seemed to be crushed by Absalom's rebellion. Now he pleads for mercy and receives it. David's kingdom is to be a kingdom of mercy. There is to be plenty of room for restored rebels. David will even protect people like Shimei against the claims of revenge. Abishai feels Shimei should be executed. It would have been understandable if David had agreed. But so much does David want his kingdom to be a kingdom of mercy, he defends Shimei and gives him a sworn promise. Under David's kingdom he will always be safe (19:18b–23). So it is with us. In the kingdom of Jesus, our Saviour will forever keep us safe from the revenge that justice could rightly execute against us.

4. **David does something that lets everyone know that his renewed kingdom will be a kingdom of justice**. Mephibosheth comes with a story that is quite different from the one that Ziba had told (19:24–30; see 16:1–4). He had deliberately been in mourning while David's kingdom had been in peril (19:24). He had wanted to support David but had been betrayed and slandered by Ziba (19:25–27a). He is now utterly trusting David's investigation and decision (19:27b–28). David's reply in 2 Samuel 19:29 is a **test** and may be compared to Solomon's decision in 1 Kings 3:25. Mephibosheth passes the test by revealing that all that matters to him is David's safe return (19:30). His story is accepted as true. David showed mercy to Ziba. He had a general policy of showing mercy. Mephibosheth's offer (19:30) was accepted, and his character was vindicated. 1 Samuel 21:7 (*'The king spared Mephibosheth'*) is a hint that Mephibosheth remained in David's favour.

Another aspect of the justice of David's kingdom is seen in Barzillai. David is eager to reward him. Barzillai asks that his son Chimham should be honoured instead, and David gave him his request (2 Samuel 19:31–39). David returns over the

Jordan (19:40). Like Jesus his new kingdom is a kingdom of God's grace, a kingdom of forgiveness, a kingdom of justice. Like David, Jesus is a King who is worthy of our return to him.

Chapter 30

Living Under Pressure
(2 Samuel 19:41–20:26)

David had many troubles. Some of them were the result of his sin against Uriah. God may allow the consequences of our own sins to work themselves out, not because he is angry with us but so that we might learn to keep away from sin. David was still facing pressures and anxieties.

1. **David faces another rebellion that ought never to have happened**. It begins with a foolish quarrel (2 Samuel 19:41–43). The Israelites criticise the Judeans (19:41). The Judeans claim special relationship to David (19:42). The Israelites then insist they have a greater claim on David than the Judeans. The Judeans reply harshly (19:43). A troublemaker named Sheba happens to be present, and in no time at all another rebellion is taking place. The Israelites desert David; only the Judeans are supporting him (2 Samuel 20:1–2).

Sometimes when there is a remarkable combination of circumstances we are impressed with the 'providence' of God. We are astonished at a string of circumstances that fit together to bring about God's will. But at times the devil seems to have his 'providence' also! A remark that never should have been made (19:42). A trouble-maker 'happens' to be there (20:1). It seems to be an event that never should have happened.

2. **David is still handling problems that arise from past situations**. Absalom had taken the concubines of David. David has to meet their needs and care for their future as widows (20:3). He is still facing complicated situations that arise out of things that happened some time ago.

103

3. **David faces what seems to be a repetition of the past**. He sends Amasa to put down the rebellion, but Amasa takes his time (20:4–5). David is alarmed. *'Sheba . . . will do more harm than Absalom'* (20:6). This is not true at all. But when you have been through a painful situation, it leaves an emotional scar. Anything that reminds you of it causes alarm. You react instinctively with fear, 'No, not that again!'

4. **David has a general he could not handle**. Again and again, Joab has simply ignored David's orders. There was not much David could do about it. Joab had sufficient power to be able to disregard David's wishes. Joab will not tolerate his being replaced by Amasa and murders him (20:7–10a). It is not difficult for him to get back the support of the army.

Why does God allow such trials to come upon his servant?

1. **They were part of the chastening for the murder of Uriah**. David had been forgiven but his sin was still bringing its consequences. An easy life had led David into sin (11:1–2). Now a complex life kept him from such easy days and easy ways.

2. **God was teaching David to live without panic**. God had delivered David many times before. David is alarmed at Sheba's rebellion (2 Samuel 20:6) but actually this rebellion will be put down without a battle. David needs to continue to get used to the idea that God will deliver him again and again. Sometimes we want God to deliver us **from** pressure, but God wants to give us peace **in pressure**. We need to learn to turn our lives over to Jesus amidst strains and stresses. We need to keep to the will of God for our lives so that we are realistic about what we can handle. Then we learn how to handle strain by confident prayer and not by panic.

In this particular case, the rebellion simply came to nothing. Joab pursued Sheba (20:10b). Amasa's body was covered up and the troops followed Joab (20:11–13). The chase of Sheba took them to Abel Beth Maacah in the far north (20:14). The city was besieged (20:15a), but a wise woman negotiates with Joab and the city does not think Sheba is worth protecting (20:15b–22). His rebellion is short-lived.

At this point the main story of 1 and 2 Samuel comes to an

end. 2 Samuel 20:23–26 lists David's officials, as a way of closing the story. The four following chapters are a series of appendices. There are two further narratives (2 Samuel 21:1–14; 24:1–17) about events in David's life. It is only in 1 Kings that we shall have the end of the story and learn of David's intervention to secure Solomon's succession (1 Kings 1:1–53) and his last charge to Solomon (1 Kings 2:1–9). Then we shall be told *'David rested with his fathers ... Solomon sat on the throne of David ... '* (1 Kings 2:10 & 12).

This means that the story has brought us to the end of the many events that chastised and rebuked David after his sin against Uriah. The prediction of 2 Samuel 12:11. *'I will raise up calamity against you from your own household'*, has been fulfilled. The rebellion of Sheba was the last in that series of tribulations. David was now settled securely on his throne again.

He was in his sixties. He reigned for forty years (2 Samuel 5:4). Absalom was born to a wife whom David married after he became king, and was probably in his twenties at the time of his rebellion. The two years of 13:23, the three years of 13:38, the two years of 14:28, and the four years of 15:7 (not forty; see NIV), all add up to another eleven years. So David had been reigning for over thirty years at the time of Absalom's rebellion. He died aged about seventy after a forty year reign. At the end of 2 Samuel 20:22 he is therefore in his sixties.

The point we are left with, then, is that the promise of chapter 7 will be fulfilled. No rebellion, no crisis, will ever destroy the promise of God to David. The rebellion of Sheba was simply an intimidation from the devil (as we may say, looking at it in the light of New Testament knowledge). But it came to nothing. Once God has given his promises we can inherit them by faith and patience. Once God has given his oath, the promises have been obtained and cannot be lost. David had received the oath of God. He made some bad mistakes but God disciplined him and stayed with him. It was a firmly settled matter; Jesus would be the 'Son of David'.

Chapter 31

Gibeonites and Philistines
(2 Samuel 21:1–22)

The last four chapters of 2 Samuel are a series of appendices to the story that has been told so far. There are six sections in it. There is a narrative (2 Samuel 21:1–14), a list (21:15–22) and a song (22:1–51), followed in the opposite order by a song (23:1–7), a list (23:8–39) and a narrative (24:1–25).

The incident of the Gibeonites (2 Samuel 21:1–14) is mentioned first. At some stage in the story of David there had been famine for three years. David enquired from God what the cause of it was and discovered God was grieved with the sin of Israel because of an occasion when Saul had sought to exterminate the Gibeonites (21:1). The Gibeonites had been incorporated into Israel but they were not part of Israel originally. The background to their story is in Joshua chapter 9, recalled in 2 Samuel 21:2. Israel had made a treaty with them and they were incorporated into Israel. Saul had evidently wanted to slaughter and exterminate the entire people. Yet an oath had been sworn to them. God regarded such a public betrayal of an oath, added to a racist desire to exterminate a whole people, as a serious breach of justice. The calamity of a three year famine forced the nation to attend to the matter.

David tells the Gibeonites he is willing to make amends (21:3) and they explain that financial compensation is not really sufficient and revenge is not within their power (21:4). They are hinting that only David can deal with the matter, and he accepts their hint and undertakes to do whatever is needed. They suggest that since Saul was the one who sought to exterminate them, seven of his family should be executed as a token of justice towards the Gibeonites (21:5–6). This is what was done (21:7–9). A daughter of Saul protected the bodies from being dishonoured (21:10) and eventually the bodies were given honourable burial and the remains of Saul and Jonathan were honourably buried at the same time. Then the famine ended (21:11–14). It is a strange story, yet there are some important principles in it.

1. **The story is an indication of how seriously God takes an oath**. We have seen that God made a covenant with David that his line would last for ever. But Israel also made a covenant with the Gibeonites. If God is to take his covenant-promises seriously, then Israel must realise what a serious matter covenant-making is.

2. **The story reveals how God hates injustice towards a subservient people**. The Gibeonites would be a despised people with Israel. But God did not despise them. When obligations to them were disregarded, God acted.

3. **The story reveals that justice has to be done publicly**. The precise way the Gibeonites were honoured is painful. Why, we ask, should innocent people die because of a past sin? The innocent members of Saul's family should be treated with honour for losing their lives for the sake of justice in the land of Israel. That innocent people sometimes die in a war is often accepted as inevitable among modern people. That innocent people might have to die for internal necessities of a nation's justice is less familiar to modern people but was taken as a matter of course in the ancient world.

David seeks to bring justice and unity to his nation. He discovers that Rizpah is also concerned about the honour of her family. David not only publicly makes amends to the Gibeonites, he also publicly honours Saul's family as well. The story is a strange one to our ears but it underlines the importance in every community – including modern nations and the church of Jesus Christ – of satisfying the people's sense of justice.

The last battles with the Philistines are mentioned next, plus a list of David's heroes (2 Samuel 21:15–22). The story is included because it mentions the last time David was engaged in battle with the Philistines. In many ways these heroes make us think of Jesus.

1. We see **a king who was indispensable to his people**. David went out to battle and nearly got killed (21:15–17). He was getting older and it took a speedy rescue by Abishai to save David from being killed. The people at that point decided that David should no more be involved in warfare with the Philistines *'so that the lamp of Israel will not be extinguished'*. Sometimes, when we read the story of Old Testament figures like David, they help us to deepen our understanding of Jesus because they resemble him. Sometimes they help us to see Jesus because they are a contrast to him. In this case David contrasts with Jesus. Jesus is our David, our perpetually burning Lamp empowered by the oil of the Spirit, One who will never be extinguished.

2. We see **a king who accomplished his task**. There were two more battles with the Philistines (21:18, 19) and then they never seem to have attacked Israel again. One of the goals of David's lifelong ministry as king of Israel was completed. He had thoroughly defeated the Philistines. David's earliest call to serve God came as a call to defeat Philistines. He had become famous when he defeated Goliath. But his men followed in his steps. They were willing to fight with giants. A nephew of David killed Ishbi-Beniob (21:16–17). Sibbecai killed Saph (21:18). Elhanan killed Goliath (21:19; this Goliath seems to have been brother to the famous 'Goliath'; see 1 Chronicles 20:5). Another nephew of David, named Jonathan, killed a giant with twenty-four fingers and toes (21:20–21). He could not bear that Israel should be taunted. Including the famous Goliath, the giants amounted to five in the same family (21:22). No wonder David had five stones in his sling!

So now that the last battle with the Philistines had been fought his calling in this area is accomplished. He had fought a good fight. He had finished the journey. He endured to the end. For the joy that was set before him, he continued until his work was accomplished.

Chapter 32

The Lord is My Rock
(2 Samuel 22:1–28)

The appendices to the main story-line of Samuel have two songs. In 2 Samuel 22:1–51 we have a song of praise in which David worships God for the many victories he has given him.

Perhaps it was written after the occasion mentioned in 2 Samuel 21:17 when David realised he would never again go out to war.

1. **It begins with praise for the protection of God** (22:2–4). He uses a mixture of descriptions of God. Some of the descriptions are impersonal. God is a 'Rock', a place which cannot be shaken or burned or easily destroyed. David had hidden behind literal rocks (1 Samuel 23:25) but finds God is a greater protection. God is a 'Fortress', a place where one is safe from invaders. Adullam had been a fortress (1 Samuel 22:4) but the true Fortress was God himself. God is a 'Shield', a means of protection when missiles are being thrown. He is a 'Horn', the powerful part of a wild animal used to repel enemies. He is a 'Refuge' or 'High Tower', a place of retreat and safety.

Two of the descriptions are personal. God is a 'Deliverer' and a 'Saviour'.

The child of God is, like David, surrounded by many enemies. Satan is the ultimate enemy, perhaps unknown to David, but for the modern Christian known to be the inventor behind the evil circumstances and attacks that trouble us. But the Christian can praise God that he is in a place of total safety with a powerful Deliverer.

109

2. **David rejoices in his being kept safe from the ultimate enemy, death** (2 Samuel 22:5–7). There had been times when David had been like a drowning man. The waves of death had almost overwhelmed him. The floods of destruction were all around him (2 Samuel 22:5). Death seemed to have ropes and traps with which to catch him and hold him fast (22:6). Satan wants to kill us in one way or another, at least to kill our usefulness or to smother our testimony. But God is our Protector. His protection comes as we pray. David often has occasion to call out to God (2 Samuel 22:4 and 22:7). God's rescuings come in answer to our prayers. God hears from his heavenly temple.

3. **David describes God's deliverances in a series of vivid pictures**. God is like a great earthquake (22:8). No one who has been even on the edge of an earthquake will ever forget it. The ground feels like water. Buildings wobble as if made of rubber. People scream and rush into the streets. When David has been rescued by God it is as if everything turns to instability when God appears. God is like blazing fire (22:9). He consumes and annihilates all sin. Everything lacking substance or worth is shrivelled.

He comes like **a warrior in a chariot**. *'He opened up the heavens also, and came down'* (22:10). Darkness is beneath his feet. The clouds are his chariot-throne, which is carried or accompanied by supernatural beings, 'cherubs'. The wind carries him wherever he wishes to go (22:11). His chariot has a covering of darkness over it. *'He set darkness around him. His canopy was the thick clouds of the rain-waters'* (2 Samuel 22:12).

He is like a **mighty storm out at sea**. Burning hail falls from the skies (22:13). God thunders from heaven (22:14). He sends out arrows of lightning (22:15). The waters rise and fall and it seems as if the sources of the waters and the very foundations of the earth will become visible from beneath the waves (22:16). Amidst such a mighty terrifying storm, God reaches out and takes hold of his servant and keeps him safe (22:17).

This is all David's picture-language as he tries to describe the rescuings of God. Many times he has been delivered from his enemies by dramatic interventions of God (22:18). They attacked him when he was in trouble but God was always there to rescue him (22:19). David was not merely one who barely survived. He was given great victory. He was brought out into a large and spacious place where he had freedom and liberty and room to move (22:20).

4. **David claims that God has rescued him because David is righteous** (2 Samuel 22:22–28). David's words are not a claim to a purity of character that can stand before God's judgement. Rather they are a claim that he is in the work of God and his cause is a just and righteous one. In this sense he knows that he is righteous, clean, blameless, pure, afflicted rather than haughty. No one can pray this way if he or she is seeking to claim to stand up to the demands of God as he searches our inward character. But David is not writing at this point as a sinner standing before God, but as God's king in God's work standing before enemies who wish to destroy him.

We cannot appeal to our righteousness when we are asking God to bless us as though we were without sin. But there are times when in a situation of dispute and persecution we know that our cause is basically a righteous one. It is with such a spirit that David is praising God for his deliverances. His life has sought to be one of obedience to God's written revelations, his 'ordinances' and 'statutes'. He knows that he has wanted to do God's will. He is what he is by God's grace but he knows that in situations of conflict he has been sincere of heart, and with clean hands. He knows that although our position before God is one of receiving mercy, it is also true that in those who have received mercy, God honours faithfulness and integrity.

One must remember too that there is a forward look in David's psalm. He often describes what the righteous Davidic king **ought** to be like, and in so writing looks forward to a perfect King, a Messiah. Romans 15:8–12 quotes the psalm and applies it to Jesus. The psalm points to Jesus as the great and true David, the One who is the man after God's own heart even more than David was.

Chapter 33

Praises to Your Name

(2 Samuel 22:29–51)

5. **David speaks of the great accomplishments that he has been able to achieve, entirely by the protection and help of God** (2 Samuel 22:29–30).

God has been to him like a burning oil-lamp (22:29), giving him illumination and understanding and warmth. God has inspired him with such energy that he has been able to leap over walls (22:30). Even the fortress of Zion, which was thought could not possibly be defeated, had been won. David had leaped over the wall (see 2 Samuel 5:6–7).

6. **David thinks how the way in which God had led him reveals what God is like (22:31–32).** *'His way'*, the pathway through life along which God had led him, was perfect. 'The word of the Lord' had proved utterly reliable. *'He is a shield to all who take refuge in him'*; those who trust in him find that he protects them (22:31). David rejoices in his uniqueness. There is nothing and no one like him (22:32).

7. **David thinks of the way in which God has trained him** (22:33). God had been a protection to him, and had put him on the road to all that he was called to do for God (22:33). The experiences he has had in the past have all perfectly been suited to him. He had learned lessons of faith in the fields with the sheep, and on the battlefield with Saul. His years as a fugitive had contributed to his qualifications. God had given him physical strength (22:34, *'feet like hinds' feet'*) and training for his work as king. He had been given skill in the ways of war (22:35), and then protected as he came into fame (22:36–37).

8. **David thinks of the way his training had enabled him to fulfil his calling** (2 Samuel 22:38–43). He had undertaken his work energetically and boldly, conquering God's enemies (22:38–39), conscious that God was with him (22:40–41). The prayers of the ungodly had gone unheard (22:42) and David had overcome the enemies of God's kingdom (22:43).

9. **David recalls the way God had protected his position as king** (2 Samuel 22:44–46). The *'contentions of the people'* (22:44) had not defeated him. Civil wars had been put down. There had been times of long war against him (see 2 Samuel 3:1) but David had grown steadily victorious in such situations. His position as *'head of the nations'* had been preserved. It is phrases like this that make us know David is looking and writing beyond himself. David was *'head of the nations'* in the sense of conquering some surrounding territories. But the phrase really suits One greater than David. David is only the forerunner and shadow. It is the Lord Jesus Christ who fulfils David's psalm in a greater way. He also faced the *'contentions of the people'* but God enables his kingdom to go forward and protects his position as *'Head over the nations'*. Also, it is true of Jesus even more than it was true of David that *'people I did not know'* come and subject themselves to him, either willingly (22:44) or unwillingly (22:45–46).

10. **Finally David turns again to fresh praise and worship for God's blessings and deliverances** (2 Samuel 22:47–51).

God is the living God. *'The LORD lives!'* says David (2 Samuel 22:47). It was decades previously that David had said about Goliath, *'Who is this uncircumcised Philistine that he should defy the armies of the **living** God?'* Now, many years later, he still has the same conviction. David had years to confirm that God is alive.

God is the unfailing God. The cliffs and caves in which David had hidden spoke of places that could not be moved. Saul had destroyed houses and villages but no one could move the rocks of the wilderness that David had known years previously. So he delights to call God *'my Rock'* (2 Samuel 22:47).

God is the delivering God, *'the Rock of my salvation'*. Man is such a weak frail creature, and is surrounded by so many enemies that he always needs rescuing.

God is a vindicating God (2 Samuel 22:48, 49). He brings to light sooner or later the rightness of his cause and the integrity of his servants.

David plans to *'give thanks ... among the nations'* (22:50). David is going beyond himself. How can David in himself be heard internationally? It takes a greater-than-David to fulfil such a ministry.

David in his last lines sees himself in a ministry as God's king only by virtue of the fact that God has rescued him from many enemies and many intrigues (22:51). He is *'God's anointed'* only because he is the object of God's loving-kindness.

This kingship continues by means of his descendants and his Descendant, for ever. Every aspect of this psalm suits our Lord Jesus Christ. Jesus found his Father to be a Shield, a Refuge and a 'High Tower'. Jesus not only was kept from death until the time for his cross came; he was delivered **through** death (22:2–7). He experienced God in the wonders of his deliverances (22:8–17) and had known times when he needed protection from his enemies (22:18–19). He was the One exalted as king of the nations and brought into a *'spacious place'* as ruler of the universe (22:20). More than David he could claim that God had rescued him because he was *'the Righteous One'* (22:21–28). He had accomplished salvation for the nations by the enabling of the Father (22:29–30) and had proved and revealed what God is like (22:31–32). Even the young boy Jesus had learned obedience through the things he suffered and had been perfectly equipped by the Father, protected as he came into fame (22:33–37), enabled by the Spirit to fulfil his calling (22:38–43), shielded (22:44–46), and enabled to do his entire work *'to the glory of God the Father'* (22:47–51).

The privilege of sovereignty under God began with David but then was handed down from generation to generation until it reached Jesus; then God gave him *'the throne of his father David'* (Luke 1:32).

Chapter 34

David's Last Words
(2 Samuel 23:1–7)

The second of the two songs in the appendices to the book of
Samuel is called *'the last words of David'* (2 Samuel 23:1–7).
This probably does not mean the 'last words' David ever
uttered, but last words that he wrote among his many psalms.

1. **He describes himself** (2 Samuel 23:1). He is *'the man who
was raised up on high'*. He is conscious of God's sovereignty.
What was done through David was not simply his own
power. God had created him. God made him the person that
he was in his temperament, his circumstances, his background. Even the fact that he was *'son of Jesse'* was part of
God's plan.

He is *'anointed of God'*. The plan of God cannot go forward
in anyone's life until there is the enabling of the Holy Spirit.
David's life work was done because there was a time when
Samuel poured oil over him and the Spirit came upon him
from that day forward (1 Samuel 16:13).

He is the *'sweet psalmist of Israel'*. It is notable that when
David is wanting to describe himself, the item that he singles
out for mention is his contribution to the music and worship
of Israel. He could have mentioned the defeat of the Philistines or the capture of Jerusalem, but in his mind his greatest
contribution to Israel was in his psalms.

2. **He is conscious of his inspiration** (2 Samuel 23:2–3a).
'The spirit of the LORD spoke by me...'. David was aware
that in his many songs he had been given inspiration. He
knows that his words have come from a source higher than
human creativity. God has been giving the gift of prophecy.

115

His words have been God's words. He is conscious that he **knows** he has been verbally inspired as he has written many of his compositions. *'His Word has been on my tongue'*. David knows about the strange combination of the divine and the human as the Word of God is given. It is *'His Word'*, but it is *'my tongue'*. Man is speaking; God is speaking. There is a mysterious intertwining of the human and divine. David has been saying what he wants to say. Yet at the same time it has been *'the God of Israel . . . the Rock of Israel'* who has been speaking in him.

3. **He defines the character of his reign** (2 Samuel 23:3b–4). He had to be like God himself, ruling *'in righteousness'* and *'in the fear of God'*. True leadership has to be just and fair. It has to uphold the standards of mercy and equality that are to be found in God's dealing with humankind. It has also to be mindful of the judgement of God and his determination that justice and truth prevail.

A king who rules in such a way *'is like the light of morning at sunrise'* (2 Samuel 23:4). He brings **light**. There is illumination and understanding. There is the end of darkness and obscurity. He brings **warmth**. People can relax and enjoy life. There is no need to hide or withdraw into emptiness or obscurity. Such a king brings **provision**. With light and warmth come the rains, so vital in lands like ancient Israel dependent on agriculture for their survival. David felt that the reign of the ideal king was like the time when the grass springs out of the earth.

In these pictures David is describing an ideal. They are fulfilled in Jesus. He is the light; he is warmth to our hearts; he is the source of every provision. He is God's perfect king.

4. **He sees his reign in the light of the covenant-promise to him** (2 Samuel 23:5).

> *'For is it not this way in my house in relation to God?*
> *For he made with me an everlasting covenant*
> *Ordered in all things and sure*
> *For all my salvation and all His purpose –*
> *Will he not cause it to grow?'*

David speaks of his 'house' rather than of himself person-ally. What he says he believes will come to be true through his family in days to come. The word 'covenant' did not come in 2 Samuel 7, but 2 Samuel 23:5 is the confirmation that the promises given there are covenant-promises, sworn by an oath (see also Psalm 89).

He knows that the promises given to him are fixed and settled. They cannot be lost. David's work of forwarding salvation and God's 'desire' or 'purpose' will flourish in the line of David.

It is this theme in the Bible that is the background to the coming of Jesus as the Son of David. Jesus is the heir of all of the promises to David. The promises continued in the line of David until there came One who was able to fulfil them, Jesus the Son of God. They were certain of fulfilment from the point mentioned in 2 Samuel 7 and onwards. Once God has taken a covenant-oath his purpose is *'ordered in all things and sure'*. This Davidic promise is still going forward. Jesus is still the Davidic king. He still reigns and will continue to do so until all enemies have been put beneath his feet. The conquer-ing of the world for righteousness is *'ordered in all things and sure'*. Jesus is a second David. He will conquer the world for God in a kingdom of righteousness and peace. In Jesus' hands God will cause his kingdom to grow.

5. **The godless will be removed from God's perfect kingdom** (2 Samuel 23:6–7). They are useless and dangerous, like thorns that cannot be handled. Contact with them brings no blessing. They can only be approached by one who is thor-oughly armed. Their destiny is to be removed from God's kingdom utterly. It is with this vision in his heart that David closes his ministry of song and poetry to Israel. The final kingdom will contain no sinners. God's kingdom will eventu-ally bring in perfect righteousness. It will last for ever. For those are allied to God's kingdom, the future is ordered in all things and sure.

Chapter 35

Trusting in God Alone
(2 Samuel 23:8–24:17)

The list of David's mighty men (2 Samuel 23:8–39) is followed by the story of how he numbered the fighting men of the nation (2 Samuel 24:1–25). We read of three models of courage: Josheb who killed eight hundred in one battle (2 Samuel 23:8), Eleazar who persisted in battle when others had withdrawn (23:9–10) and Shammah who defended food supplies when other Israelites had fled (23:11–12).

At one point in the cave of Adullam when David was wishing for a drink from the well in Bethlehem, three men daringly smuggled themselves through enemy lines to bring David water from Bethlehem (23:13–16a). He would not drink it but used it as a *'drink-offering'* (a ceremonial expression of dedication to God). He would not do anything that seemed to disparage the value of the lives of his men (23:16b–17). The story speaks both of the courage of the men and of the way David inspired loyalty.

Next we are told of Abishai, chief of the Thirty (23:18–19) and three of Benaiah's famous deeds (23:20–23). 2 Samuel 23:24–31 mentions sixteen more names. Verses 32–33 mention Eliahba the Shaalbonite, Jashen the Gizonite, Jonathan ... Ahiam, four names in all.[1] 2 Samuel 23:34–35 mentions another four, and, 23:36 mentions Igal and Bani the Gadite.[1] Verses 37–39a mention another five. The three of 23:8–12, Abishai and Benaiah in 23:18–23, the thirty-one names of 23:24–39 plus one more, Joab the commander, bring the total to thirty-seven (23:39). After this chapter, the story of David's counting the fighting men of the nation (2 Samuel 24:1–25) is surprising.

1. **David was falling into pride and self-sufficiency**. It was Israel who sinned first (2 Samuel 24:1). The nation had become proud of its eminence under David's leadership. It was now a large empire. The entire nation felt self-confident, as if they had personally been able to get to where they were. God became angry and David was allowed to fall into the same sin. In pride and boastfulness David decided to count the fighting men of the nation to show how powerful the nation was (2 Samuel 24:2). It was a military census (2 Samuel 24:9). David assesses his strength wrongly.

He is forgetting his strength came entirely from God. Chapter 23 said as much. David's counting the warriors of Israel came to a total of 1.3 million men. But when we look at the mighty deeds of 2 Samuel 23:8–39, how many had God needed? Thirty-seven! David was forgetting the lessons of his own history. He had not needed 1.3 million. The mightiest exploits of the nation had not been achieved by great numbers; they had been achieved by a few men who were great in faith. He is forgetting the very titles he had used for God on a previous occasion. He had once sung about God as his fortress and his deliverer, and of times when he had cried for help and God had delivered him (2 Samuel chapter 22). He is also forgetting his own past. He has forgotten how he himself slew Goliath. There were hundreds of soldiers around him when David killed Goliath. But David had not got any help from the hundreds of men. The victory had come through his faith in God.

2. **David ignored a warning**. Joab protested against the census (2 Samuel 24:3). He was not a greatly spiritual man but he could see David's pride and knew no blessing would come through counting the fighting men of the nation. But David insisted (2 Samuel 24:4a) and nearly ten months were spent in collecting the information (24:4b–8). David had ignored the advice of his military commander. The figures amounted to 1.3 million fighting men (24:9). They were

collected separately for northern Israel and for Judah in the south. The fact that the figures were kept distinct shows there was still a large amount of disunity in the two parts of the nation. This was a bigger problem than any military weakness. In boasting of his military strength against outside enemies David was forgetting something that should have kept him humble.

3. **David was forgiven but was invited to consider carefully what he had done**. He soon realised that he had sinned, and came to speedy repentance. He saw it himself without any word from any other person. David's relationship with God was such that he was able to tell when he had displeased the Lord. He asked for forgiveness and fully confessed his foolishness (2 Samuel 24:10). The next day God sent a prophet to invite David to choose three possible chastening judgements which would teach David the seriousness of what he had done. It is not that David has to be punished for his sin, but sometimes our sin has to have some kind of consequence otherwise the seriousness of what we have done does not grip our hearts.

What is unusual is that David was given a choice in the matter. Why should this be? It seems that God wanted David to give time and thought to reflecting upon what he had done (24:11–13). *'Now consider…'* (24:13) is a key phrase. There were lessons to be learned if David gave more thought to the sin that he had committed and to why God was specially displeased with it. To invite David to consider various judgements would compel him to give time to the matter.

It is noticeable that all three of the judgements involved a serious loss of numbers. David had gloried in the number of fighting men. Now they would be reduced. He was offered the choice of a judgement via nature (famine) or via people (pursuit by enemies) or a judgement more directly from God (pestilence from the Lord through the activity of an angel). Any one of them would reduce the numbers of his fighting men. If David gave time to considering this matter, he would discover that to glory in human ability displeases God. He also was led to plead for God's mercy and to discover more of the great compassion of God (24:14–17).

Footnote

[1] There are textual problems in verses 32–36 but these readings are probably right.

Chapter 36

Looking Towards the Cross

(2 Samuel 24:18–25)

The lengthy book of 1–2 Samuel comes to an end with a fore-shadowing of the temple being built in Jerusalem.

God gives instructions that an altar should be built (2 Samuel 24:18). The very place is a matter of detailed instruction from God (24:19). At that time the place was owned by a man called Araunah, who seems to be a humble farmer. One day, as Araunah is working, he sees the king coming with his group of servants (24:20). He discovers the king wants to buy his land (24:21) and so offers the land and everything else that might be needed as well (24:22–23). But David would not offer a sacrifice that cost nothing (24:24). He paid the price, built the altar and offered the sacrifice. The heaven-sent plague was stopped (24:25). The story is a hint of the salvation that is coming, in the very place where the events are taking place.

1. The **reason for sacrifice** is that sin has been committed and the judgement cannot be held back without sacrifice. David's sin of pride and self-sufficiency gave rise to the entire situation. Similarly it is our pride and self-sufficiency and refusal to heed warnings that leads us into needing a Saviour. The problem of sin is so great that it is a problem even to God himself. Sin has consequences. In some mysterious way it appears that even God cannot say 'We'll just forget it'. His wrath against sin is necessary. He has an instinctive holy antagonism towards sin. He must punish it. His anger is not

122

personal malice. It is not something out of control. It is not his 'losing' his temper. But sin is so severe, it requires sacrifice and bloody compensation. This may be offensive to 'modern man' but it is the gospel. The plague would not stop without sacrifice for sin.

2. The **type of sacrifice** is the shedding of blood, as a means of payment and compensation for sin. Men and women would like to have some other way of compensating for sin. Some bring their good works and their pleasant character, but nothing will make up for the sin we have committed. The sacrifices needed in this story included the whole burnt offering. The entire animal was offered up to God as a symbol of total sacrifice, total dedication. The sacrifices included also the peace-offerings, the shedding of blood and the offering of the animal, but the leaving of a part of it for eating and celebrating. It symbolised reconciliation and fellowship as the result of blood-sacrifice. But without the shedding of blood there was no forgiveness. So it is with our Saviour. Without the shedding of his blood, there was nothing that could deal with sin. He had to die in our place.

3. The **painfulness of sacrifice** is emphasised. It has to be costly. A cheap offering will not do. Araunah was a dedicated and generous man and was loyal to his king. He was quite willing to somehow relieve David of any cost to himself. But David felt he could not accept such an offer. No doubt it was his own feeling of guilt that made him react in the way he did. He had the feeling in his heart that a sacrifice for sin should in some way be costly. The feeling is right, but in the case of Our Lord Jesus the cost was not imposed on us; it was inflicted on Jesus. It is beyond our ability to conceive what he endured by way of sufferings as the cost of the atoning for our sins. Pain, indignity, ridicule, abandonment, injustice, and worst of all, abandonment by the Father, all added their weight to what he bore for us.

4. The **place of sacrifice** is a place in Jerusalem, on Mount Moriah. Araunah's field became the site of the temple. It was the place where blood-sacrifice would be offered day after day, year after year, for centuries. It was also the place where

Abraham had *'spared not his own son but delivered him up'* at least in intent if not in actuality. A thousand years later in those very localities Jesus would be examined in the high priest's house. There he would be disowned by his leading apostle. There he would be accused of destroying the temple that would be on that very spot. There he would be degraded in a dozen ways. There he would be stripped and executed as God's whole burnt offering for our sins, as God's peace offering. God spared not his own son but delivered him up for us all.

5. The **result of the sacrifice** is reconciliation. When the sacrifice for David's sin was offered the plague stopped. The compulsory enmity within the heart of God towards sin is somehow placated by the sacrifice of his Son. The sacrifices of the Old Testament and of stories like this one are but feeble pictures. The subject is mysterious but what we know is that the result of the cross of Jesus Christ, when received in faith, is reconciliation. We are no longer alienated from God, no longer at a distance from him. Rather, he is able to pour his love into our hearts. The 'plague' of his wrath stops and the flow of his love is communicated to us. He makes us his children. He takes us into his arms. We are at peace within his love. God becomes tangibly and obviously our friend, our Father, our Saviour.

And so the book of 1 and 2 Samuel comes to a close pointing to Jesus. For our sins were the reason for his sacrifice. His blood was the means of my forgiveness. He paid the price we could not pay. In Jerusalem was a place where God, like Abraham on Mount Moriah, spared not his own Son. And mine was the benefit, eternal reconciliation with the Father.

> I had a debt I could not pay.
> He paid a debt He did not owe.
> I needed someone to wash my sins away.
> And now I sing a brand new song – amazing grace!
> Christ Jesus paid the debt that I could never pay.

Appendix

Some Facts About 1 and 2 Samuel

Matters of 'Introduction' do not receive detailed discussion in this book but there are a few basic facts which we ought to know.

The books of 1 and 2 Samuel are actually only one book in the Hebrew original. It was apparently first divided into two books by the Greek translators in the third century BC.

'Samuel' is a book full of stories telling us of the rise of kingship in Israel. This is important to us because much of the Bible is concerned about kingship or kingdom. If you were to put into one word the message of the Bible, what would that word be? It could be 'gospel' – good news. It could be 'salvation'. It could be 'reconciliation'. But probably the best single word that summarises the entire message of the Bible is the word 'kingdom'. It was the word Jesus used to summarise his message. Jesus could have come preaching 'The gospel is at hand', or 'Salvation is at hand'. But the way he chose to put his message was to say *'The kingdom is at hand'*.

Jesus is a king. His powerful work in this world is called 'kingdom'. He makes us to reign and rule with him, so we are kings and priests unto God. His kingdom has come, his kingdom is coming, his kingdom will come. These are the themes of the Bible. It is this that is behind the stories of the books of Samuel and of Kings. They are the story of the rise of God's kingdom in Israel. From them we learn much about God's kingdom as it operates in our times and in our lives.

Five questions will lead us into what we need to know about 1 and 2 Samuel.

Who wrote it? We do not know precisely, but it seems that the book of Deuteronomy kept on being enlarged with historical supplements which were written in the same style as the book of Deuteronomy, which itself comes mainly from the days of Moses. At one point there must have been Deuteronomy-Joshua. Then it got enlarged a bit more and there was Deuteronomy-Joshua-Judges, something like an expanded Deuteronomy, a third edition of Israel's history, all written in the same style. Then there was a 'fourth edition', Deuteronomy-Joshua-Judges-Samuel. Then finally there was Deuteronomy-to-2-Kings, all written in the 'Deuteronomic' style and all building upon the teaching of the book of Deuteronomy.

When was it written? It seems that 1, 2 Samuel as we have it has to be dated after the division of Israel into two kingdoms in about 970 BC (because of 1 Samuel 27:6). So probably Deuteronomy-to-2-Samuel existed as a history of Israel in about 950 BC. The full story Deuteronomy-to-2-Kings was completed later in the sixth century as a kind of 'fifth edition' of Israel's history.

Why was it written? The wise men and prophets of Israel felt it useful to keep a record of the things God had done within Israel's history. So, under the inspiration of the Holy Spirit they felt led to compile this history for the benefit of later ages.

How was it written? The author-editor of Samuel used sources. Some fragments of history had already been written and an author-editor put it all together. Some scholars think they can reconstruct what the sources were. They may be right, but it is hard to prove the scholars are doing anything more than guessing.

How does the story unfold? 'Samuel' – a single book in the Hebrew – gives us story after story concerning how David came to be king. Those who like stories should like 'Samuel'.

It focuses on one person after another. First we meet Hannah and discover how Samuel came to be born (1 Samuel 1:1–2:10), then we read about the events of Shiloh, how Eli's household was faithless and how it was replaced by Samuel's ministry (2:11–4:1a). Then we read about how the ark was lost (1 Samuel 4:1b–7:2) and then twenty years later was recovered (7:3–17). Chapters 8 to 15 deal with the people's demand for a king, their being given Saul, and the eventual failure of Saul through disobedience.

Then the book gets really exciting. We read about David and his early life (16–20) and his life as an outlaw with king Saul hunting for him (21–27). Chapters 28–31 tell us of Saul's final days.

In what we call '2 Samuel' David hears the news of Saul's death (chapter 1) and is made king (chapter 2) but for a few chapters he is still not king of all Israel. There is civil war between David's supporters and followers of Saul (chapters 3–4). Finally David becomes king of all Israel at Hebron, Jerusalem becomes his capital city, he defeats the Philistines and establishes his empire (5:1–9:13). At that point David almost ruins his life. There is a time of war with Ammon (10:1–19). At such a time David commits adultery but is rebuked by God through Nathan, and (although he is forgiven) terrible problems are predicted for his life (11:1–12:31). Chapters 13–19 tell of the immense conflicts he had within his own family and nation. Chapters 21–24 tell of his warriors (chapter 21), his music (chapter 22), his last words (chapter 23) and his self-confidence in numbering the people.

The books of Samuel do not tell of David's death and the handing of the kingdom to Solomon. These come in the early chapters of the books of Kings.

More Advanced Reading

In 1 Samuel (pp. 124–127) I have referred to some books which give help for the more advanced reader, including the best commentaries on 1–2 Samuel. The remarks I made there continue except that I can mention that G.J. Keddie's

Triumph of the King (Evangelical Press) covers 2 Samuel and is good for those who speak English as a foreign language. W.G. Blaikie's *The Second Book of Samuel* (reprinted by Klock & Klock) continues his earlier volume on 1 Samuel. Heavily academic works covering 2 Samuel are A.A. Anderson's *2 Samuel* (Word) and P.K. McCarter's *II Samuel* (Doubleday).